The Roaring Twenties . . .

Prohibition was five years old. In New York City alone 5,000 nightclubs, newly called speakeasies, were selling questionable Scotch at $20 a quart to a clamoring public. Young men wearing silk shirts had just heard themselves called "flaming youth" and were doing their best to live up to the name.

Autographed slickers, raccoon coats and ukeleles were current fads, while people danced the Charleston to "Charlie My Boy," and "Limehouse Blues," played on crank-up phonographs.

One brisk afternoon, a 19-year-old hayseed, in a loud plaid suit, clutching a dented silver cornet, came to the city. Loring Nichols of Utah was approaching one of the most fabulous careers in the whole fabulous world of Jazz. . . .

The Five Pennies

By GRADY JOHNSON

*The Biography of
Jazz Band Leader Red Nichols*

Containing a novelization of Dena Pictures'
Paramount Release in VistaVision ® and Technicolor ®

THE FIVE PENNIES

Starring DANNY KAYE and
BARBARA BEL GEDDES, LOUIS ARMSTRONG,
HARRY GUARDINO, BOB CROSBY, BOBBY TROUP

*Screenplay by Jack Rose and Melville Shavelson
Story by Robert Smith*

A DELL FIRST EDITION
an original book

Published by
DELL PUBLISHING CO., INC.
750 Third Avenue
New York 17, N.Y.

© Copyright, 1959, by Paramount Pictures Corporation

All rights reserved

Designed and produced by
Western Printing & Lithographing Company

First printing—May, 1959

Printed in U.S.A.

BACKSTAGE...

One morning in November, 1958, Loring "Red" Nichols, a smiling, dimpled, brown-eyed little jazz band leader with graying red hair, a florid face and an ample Irish nose, walked onto a huge darkened sound stage at Paramount Pictures in Hollywood, California, ill-at-ease because he had been invited to see certain poignant events of his life pass before his eyes in a motion picture being filmed there.

On his left, as he picked his way over light power cables in the semi-darkness, was a row of green portable dressing rooms. Their doors were open and light spilled from them. The first dressing rooms were small cubes and the names of their occupants were crudely chalked on the doors as though they were of no great importance. Next to them the rooms were larger bungalows with peaked roofs, the occupants' names properly printed on white cards at their doors. In the first of these latter sat a fat, squat Negro man, looking for all the world like a well-fed frog. The card at his door read, Louis Armstrong.

Red Nichols stopped to watch Armstrong carefully rub sweet spirits of niter on a fever blister at the corner of his mouth, then apply witch hazel to his lips and with thumb and forefinger, pull tiny pieces of dead skin from them. Satchmo, generally regarded as the world's greatest trumpet player, was going through his daily ritual of getting his leather lip ready.

A Negro secretary, wearing horn-rimmed glasses, handed mes-

sages and telegrams to Armstrong, his own bulk blocking the doorway to the neck-craning curious who milled around outside. Nichols looked over the man's shoulder, smiling his affection at Louis. Satchmo looked up. "Come in, daddy," he said, grinning.

Red, fifty-three but looking a boyish forty-five, stepped up into the dressing room and pumped Louis' hand.

"It's all set, daddy-o," Louis said, gesturing with the sweat-mop handkerchief he carries in his left hand. "Joe wants you."

Red swallowed and grinned nervously. "What are you trying to do, make me cry?" Not only was his life being glorified on film but old friends like Louis, touched by the poignancy of his story, were overpowering him with kindness, such as Louis' gesture in having his agent, Joe Glaser, take Red as a client.

"Man, when we get through with you, you gonna be a bigger cat than ever. The most." Louis' head turned toward Red. "How long since Roseland?"

Red squinted at the ceiling. "Thirty years? Thirty-three?" Then, they were playing in different bands at the Roseland Ballroom in Manhattan. Red was with Sam Lannin's, Armstrong with Fletcher Henderson's. The bands alternated with continuous music. Louis admired Red's cornet so much he'd sit on the sidelines to listen when his own band was off duty. Nichols did the same thing when Satchmo was playing. When he had first heard Louis in Chicago, Red thought he was merely good, but at Roseland thought he was the greatest.

"Long time," Louis grunted. "Glad you come dig us again. Man, this is for kicks."

Just then a phonograph began playing, "When the Saints Go Marching In." Red's and Louis' eyes met and their ears tightened. It was Louis' trumpet and Red's cornet, pre-recorded by them for the picture, coming from the adjoining room.

"Louis, you're the greatest," Red said.

"Match you for it, daddy," Louis said. "But that is the best 'Saints' I ever did and I've done a lot of 'em."

Louis finished working on his lip and together they went outside and peeked into the dressing room. Sitting next to the phonograph, a silver cornet to his lips, thin fingers working the valves, motion picture star Danny Kaye was pretending to play Nichols' part. Red and Louis watched until the record stopped.

"You've got it, Danny," Red called.

Kaye nodded for them to come in. "You know, I'm beginning to think it's me playing," he said. He continued to valve the mute instrument.

A little assistant director materialized between them. "Ready for Mr. Kaye and Mr. Armstrong," he announced.

Louis shook his head sadly. "Which reminds me," he said to Danny, "if you want this picture to play down south, don't call me 'Mr. Armstrong.' Call me Louis." He chuckled. "That's for sure."

"I'll watch that, Mr. Armstrong," Danny said, coming out. He put a hand on Louis' and Red's shoulders and the three men—two famous, the other once almost forgotten—strolled toward a patch of light at the far end of the huge hangar-like room. There catwalks were suspended on chains from the high ceiling and, from these, lights as big as barrels burned onto a nightclub which had only two walls and no ceiling. On a raised bandstand were musicians portraying Red Nichols' orchestra, the Five Pennies. Sitting across a dance floor from them at a small table were New York actress Barbara Bel Geddes and ingénue Tuesday Weld, respectively portraying Red Nichols' wife, Bobbie, and their daughter, Dorothy, crippled when she was in her teens. Danny and Louis joined them. Red stopped behind the camera crane, losing himself in a group of workmen and visitors coming offstage.

After some last-minute conferences with the director, the scene began. Kaye fingered his cornet and a playback machine produced Nichols' playing "Wail to the Winds," his theme song. Except for his "wife" and "daughter" across from him, the nightclub was almost empty. Red Nichols and his Five Pennies, starting their comeback more than a decade ago, were dying.

Suddenly and dramatically from the far end of the nightclub came the sound of Louis' trumpet. Then his velvet-gravel voice grunted out the lyrics, "Won't you come home, Bill Bailey, won't you come home?"

From the bandstand, Kaye, alerted, sang back, "I'm feelin' all alone." Then he put the cornet to his lips and blew; and by the magic of movie-making, Nichols' music came through it.

Offstage, Red Nichols watched. Tears welled in his eyes. Behind Armstrong came drummer Shelly Manne, made up to look like Red's famous old rhythmist, Dave Tough. Behind him, Bandleader Ray Anthony looked for all the world like Jimmy Dorsey, while Pianist Bandleader Bobby Troup masqueraded as Red's old-time piano player, Artie Schutt.

On they came, up onto the bandstand, one after another, slapping Kaye on the back.

Offstage, the real Red Nichols turned away. He did not want them to see him cry. He tiptoed to the door of the sound stage. He waited until the red light went off, then pushed open the heavy door and went out into the California sunlight. He had to get home to suburban Glendale early because Bobbie had told him that Dorothy and his three grandchildren were coming over. Life was being good to him on his golden anniversary. Fifty years ago, in 1908, his father had handed him a silver cornet and said, "Blow, boy."

Life had not always been good. One of the most controversial jazz men in the business, Red Nichols had seen fame come and go. He had heard jazz critics accuse him of selling out to commercialism, others say he was years ahead of his time. He had taken abuse from the marijuana-smoking "vipers," the rum pots and hop heads who thought his brand of precision jazz stank. He had risen from a sick bed to find his band taken over by another. He had reached the top and he had hit bottom. Then, when things were blackest, it seemed that God, too, had turned against him.

This is his story, with some minor incidents fictionalized but in the main true. . . .

CHAPTER 1

THE YEAR WAS 1924, six years after the end of World War I. Calvin Coolidge was serving out the late President Harding's term and ordering government departments to quit wasting pencils while telling the nation to "keep cool with Coolidge." Prohibition was five years old. In New York City alone five thousand nightclubs, newly called speakeasies, were selling questionable Scotch for twenty dollars a quart to persons not hurt by a brief but sharp depression. Young men wearing silk shirts had just heard themselves called "flaming youth" and were trying to live up to the name in these "roaring twenties."

Autographed slickers, raccoon coats, ukuleles and John Held Jr. were current fads while women were being encouraged to smoke cigarettes by ads which showed them asking men to "blow some my way."

Teapot Dome had boiled with scandal; there was a pioneering round-the-world flight by two army transport planes; and radios were getting "loud speakers" while the first coast-to-coast network boasted twenty-seven stations. Dictionaries were being put on trains to help patrons with the new crossword puzzle. On crank phonographs people played, "Does the Spearmint Lose Its Flavor on the Bedpost Overnight?," "Amapola," "Charley, My Boy," "All Alone," "I Wonder What Became of Sally?" and "Limehouse Blues." They used snappy rejoinders like "Oh, yeah?," "Says you!" and "How're your rabbits?" They practiced "autosuggestion," saying "Day by day in every way I'm getting better and better," danced the Charleston to "vulgar" jazz music, saw Valentino and Fairbanks movies, and heard Paul Whiteman invade the field of serious music with his new symphonic jazz in a concert at Aeolian Hall in New York, playing for the first time George Gershwin's "Rhapsody in Blue," with the composer at the piano.

On a brisk afternoon in the fall of that year a ferry boat pushed across the Hudson from Jersey. Its passengers lined the rail looking ahead at the massive spectacle of Manhattan's skyscrapers turning orange in the setting sun. The men wore kid gloves, spats and Homburgs, the women short dresses, small hats and fur chokers. In contrast to their fine dress, a nineteen-year-old boy wearing a loud plaid suit and cap sat on his battered upturned suitcase against the pilot house, drinking in the scenery, feeling the challenge it flung back across the water. His brown eyes glistened beneath wavy red hair while the dimples in his red cheeks softened the jut of his jaw. In his right hand was a dented silver cornet, in his left a big old-fashioned door key. He looked at the key and felt again his father putting it in his hand back home in Ogden. He heard him saying, "If the going gets rough, son, you can always come back home." The old man, his teacher, had been a martinet. Whenever Red hit a wrong note he cracked him across the knuckles with his baton. Later he whipped him with his razor strop for playing jazz, the evil music of the whorehouses and speakeasies, and had cried with the boy when the latter sobbed, "I can't help it, papa, I got to play it." When Red threatened to run away from home on a freight train, the father capitulated.

Red put the key into his pants pocket and looked ahead at the skyline over the shoulders of the well-dressed New Yorkers. The going would not be rough. Already he had an offer to form his own band to play at Pelham Heath Inn and he was on his way to accept another job until the first materialized. Someday he would wear kid gloves, Homburgs, double-breasted blue overcoats and spats, too. He might even wear a mustache and get a raccoon coat like the college boys.

Red rubbed his silver cornet on his coat sleeve, then put it to his lips. His red face swelled and became redder. A blues melody came from the horn, scudded across the water and bounced back off the buildings. It made him feel good to know that he could get an echo from a skyscraper as easily as he had from the mountains in Utah.

The New Yorkers at the rail turned, startled. Said Red, "I just want them to know I'm coming."

He had been coming for sixteen years. Music had been his life. His father, E. W. Nichols, thirteenth child of the third wife of a musician in Brigham Young's Mormon caravan to Utah, had sold a steer to buy a clarinet and had become a music instructor at Weber College and conductor of the Ogden Municipal Band. He had started his redheaded son on both the cornet and violin at the age of three and a year later gave him piano. Red had played in his father's ladies' band until he became so big that the hoots of his playmates caused him to desert it one day down an alley during a parade. And none other than Sousa himself had patted him on the head and said, "Young man, you will become a fine musician."

Red knew that. Not only did he know music, but underneath his country-boy exterior was a confidence and stage presence that experience had taught him. As a child he had traveled in a covered wagon with his father and three sisters all over Utah putting on shows with which the elder Nichols supplemented his meager income. On cold nights Nichols put heated bricks in the wagon to keep the children warm. When they reached the edge of a town the father put on a bearskin suit and Red led him on all fours down the streets advertising their show. Red was a born entertainer who had also led a Grand Army of the Republic Parade in Salt Lake City at the age of four wearing a gold-braided cap and uniform and tooting a tasseled cornet. He could stand on his feet and hold his own.

Besides he had met two young men who had influenced his music for good—Bix Beiderbecke and Miff Mole—and he had picked up some Eastern experience playing at Atlantic City and at Asbury Park, N. J., and had made an Edison record with an orchestra, a fox trot entitled "Dirty Face, Dirty Hands." In Atlantic City he had met jazz violinist Joe Venuti and guitarist

Eddie Lang and made a mental note to try to get them in his own band some day. Then at Asbury Park, with Johnny Johnson he had been promised a chance to form his own band. Johnson had found himself with two contracts which overlapped, one in Florida and one at the Pelham Heath Inn, in New York, and had suggested that if Red could put together a band he could have the latter engagement.

So now Red Nichols, with hayseed in his hair and sophistication in his horn, was ready for the big town. Despite his youth, it held no terror for him. He had been prepared well by his father and he had had good experience getting there. The ferry bumped its slip pilings. Crosswalks were put down and he walked ashore. For a moment he looked about, confused by the noise and bustle. Then, realizing this was the tempo of the music he loved, he walked on, losing himself in the big city sounds, hearing again in his mind the rhythms of Nick LaRocca and Larry Shields whose pioneer Dixieland style had come up the river from New Orleans to set the pattern for his own.

When students were persecuting and hazing him back at Culver Military Academy in Indiana because of his Mormon beliefs, Red had locked himself in his room and doodled with his muted cornet to the first records made by LaRocca and Shields' original Dixieland band. While doing it he smoked cigarettes because he thought this was necessary to make him look like a jazz musician. Caught smoking, he had been expelled and sent home, disgraced in his father's eyes, a hero to the gangs at the poolhalls.

Lights glowed in the Plaza Hotel as Red walked

along the lines of horsedrawn hansom cabs drawn up before it. He still carried his valise and his cornet and he felt vaguely uncomfortable about something. He turned and saw what it was. The horse behind him was wearing a blanket of material exactly like his jacket. The horse turned his head to stare at him. Hastily, Red moved off toward the hotel's brightly lit marquee.

He went through the revolving doors of the hotel. Inside, a chic crowd of New Yorkers surged around him. The girls' dresses were cut to their knees. Some had bobbed their hair. They wore long pearl beads and carried ostrich feather fans. They walked with a swing to their low-swung hips that he had not seen in Utah. There the proper Mormon ladies were slower to adopt the new flapper styles. Their hair was long, their dresses like the Gibson Girls'. They did not smoke cigarettes in long holders. They did not smoke at all, it being against their religion.

Remembering this and still self-conscious about his own smoking, Red dropped the cigarette he was smoking into a cuspidor. After a moment he shrugged and lit another.

In the lobby, Red stopped to inspect a huge placard. Dominating it was a portrait of a handsome, impeccably dressed young man with wavy hair. He was singing through a megaphone.

The music of Paradise, the placard read. *Wil Paradise, the sweetest melodies ever played. Rose Room.*

Red hesitated. He saw a mirror and started to comb his deep wavy hair. Passersby turned to look and he stopped, pretending to be adjusting his bow tie. He shined one of his shoes on his pants. He took out his handkerchief, folded it to the cleanest side and arranged it neatly in his pocket. He was about to enter the room when he turned back to adjust his tie once more. He paused, listening. The thin, treacly voice of a crooner came from the room. Red wagged his head in disapproval, squared his shoulders, and entered.

This was the beautiful Rose Room but now its petals were falling. Chairs and tables were stacked. The floor was littered. An old man was sweeping, a maid was pushing a vacuum cleaner over the red carpet. On the ornate bandstand Wil Paradise, the man on the placard, was singing and conducting the orchestra. Wil wore an all-day beard and a cigarette dangled from his lip. The orchestra was unkempt and sweating. Some of them had their shirts off. The drummer had a cigarette behind his ear and a bottle of needled beer on the drum. They all looked as if they'd be more at home driving a hack. Red approached the bandstand as the number came to a conclusion.

Paradise put down his megaphone and shoved his hands in his pockets. "Well, that was pretty lousy. Maybe it'll sound better with colored lights."

Red stepped up on the bandstand behind Paradise. The drummer got Wil's attention, pointed toward Red and said, "We have a visitor from the outside world—where they shave."

Wil Paradise turned and surveyed Red. "Who let you in?"

"How do you do?" Red said. "I'm Red Nichols, from Ogden, Utah. Your new cornet player, remember?"

Paradise narrowed his eyes. "You're late."

"I'm sorry, but I've never been in New York before. Did you know the BMT subway comes up here, and the IRT subway doesn't?"

Paradise stood on the balls of his feet. "Neither does the Chesapeake and Ohio, and you're the first to complain. Get your chair. Are you a sight man?"

"I can read any note that's written." Red felt that he had sounded fatuous. His voice had squeaked.

A musician whistled. The others laughed.

Paradise turned on them. "All right, you crooks, laugh. There's a new day dawning. I heard this kid out in the desert. He can play rings around any of you —and he works for half the price."

The saxophonist leered. "The sweetest music ever heard."

Red crossed to his chair, still carrying his valise. It bumped the music stands and he succeeded in knocking down several.

Paradise glared at the saxophonist. "All right, Dorsey," he said, "I've got a boy in a boiler factory in Joplin warming up for your job. So don't buy anything on time." He rapped the stand with his stick. "Okay, from the top."

Red managed to take his seat and get out his cornet. He felt uncomfortable because all the musicians were rank strangers except Dorsey. He had seen good-natured Jimmy over in Atlantic City with the Scranton Sirens. The drummer pointed to his own music for Red's benefit. "That means from here, son. And don't take the IRT."

Paradise gave the downbeat and they started to play.

Red's cornet soared out and above the band, loud and clear as a bell—a very loud bell. Paradise rapped the music stand and the musicians trailed off.

"You!" He barked at Red. "What's that town you're from?"

"Ogden, Utah."

"Well, don't play that horn so the folks back home can hear you. You've got a mute? Use it. All the time."

Red looked about him nervously. "But, Mr. Paradise—I play New Orleans style. Played it over at Atlantic City and Asbury Park. It's the newest thing." He got to his feet. "As a matter of fact"—he started to pull from his jacket some music which he and Lang and Venuti had cooked up at Atlantic City—"I have some arrangements I made of this very number. You might like to—"

"Sit down!" Paradise screamed.

"Can't you take a little friendly advice?"

"Put that horn in your big mouth and blow!"

Red sat down and blew.

He blew softly, and he blew prettily. He blew intelligently. He blew right on the nose. He didn't slide falteringly into notes or hide clinkers with riffs. He blew, they all said, like Bix Beiderbecke, with even more finesse, if less feeling, than Bix.

The drummer looked over at him when he had a break. "I'm Tony," he said. "Welcome to Paradise."

"It's all right," Red said, matter-of-factly. "Pretty soon, you'll all be working for me."

CHAPTER 2

NEW YORK would be his oyster. There he would write his name in pearly lights with his own brand of the new jazz. Already he was feeling the affluence that would be his. That night, in 1924, he was riding proudly down Broadway with his new friend, Tony, in Tony's Stutz roadster. The crisp night air stung his face and he inhaled deeply of the big town smells, of exhaust smoke, popcorn, perfume and candy stores. Lying back and looking up at the millions of lights that surrounded him, he imagined his name blinking from the marquees they passed. Between his knees beside the bucket seat of the Bearcat was the magic wand that would make all this possible—his silver cornet in its scuffed case.

Tony tooled the Stutz through the chugging traffic and pulled up beside an alleyway. Ahead was a gaudy billboard reading *Earl Carroll's Vanities*. Dominating the billboard were two of the most beautiful girls in the world. They wore feathers. Standing beneath the billboard were two very much alive creatures who might have posed for it. They wore very short dresses.

Just looking at them made Red nervous. He wanted to run to them and away from them at the same time. Tony set the hand brake and pushed his hat brim up with his thumb. "Now ain't that a sight for sore eyes?" He looked over at Red. "Which one you want? Be my guest."

Red opened the door and started to get out. "I don't think I'd better. Don't get me wrong—I appreciate it—" He started backing away. "But I hear there's a new cornet player—up in Harlem—just got in—from New Orleans—yeah, New Orleans—all the boys in the band are going up there tonight—"

"They go up every night!" Tony looked toward the girls again. "Hear him some other time. And hear these lalapaloozas tonight."

Red ducked his head to steal a glance at the girls. "Besides, I'm steering clear of chorus girls." A horse-mounted policeman passed between him and the girls and he had to stand on tiptoe to see over the horse. "My mother gave me a note to a lady she knows in Brooklyn—she's got a daughter."

"Naturally!" Tony snorted. "Brooklyn is solid mothers and daughters. Every auto horn plays Mendelssohn's 'Wedding March'—and Mendelssohn's driving the car."

"I haven't even said hello to the girl yet, and you've got me married to her!" No girl was going to hook him so easily. When he was leading his band he would have the pick of the lot. Hadn't they given him the old eye in Piquet, Ohio, Indianapolis, Chicago and Atlantic City?

"See how easy it is?" Tony spread his hands in a

hopeless gesture, then nodded to the waiting girls. "Now these Broadway frails—no home games!"

Red fixed Tony with a fishy eye. "Why are you doing all this for me? I hardly know you."

Tony shrugged elaborately. "I take in strays. I don't like anybody should be lonely. I've got a heart big as all outdoors." His heart had a sudden thought: "How much money you say you got on you?"

"Twenty bucks. Room rent."

"Forget the room. We may never have to get out of the car! Tell you what we'll do— We'll go up to Harlem—hear that horn—and from then on we'll play by ear! All right? All right!"

Before Red could stop him Tony had leaped over the door and swaggered over to the girls. Red watched him out of the corner of his eye. Tony whispered to them. The girls looked toward Red and shrugged. They started to turn away but Tony stopped them. He nodded toward Red and Red wished the sidewalk would cave in. One of the girls was blonde with curves in the forbidden places.

Red could hear her speaking: "Utah? Are they in the Union?" She laughed. "Besides, my mother warned me about musicians."

The other girl was brunette, slender and sensuous. She swept the air between her and Red with her dark lashes. He thought he heard her say, "Damp behind the ears!" The blonde, whom he already favored, now looked at his shoes. Red heard her say, "Farm boy."

Then the brunette said, "Aaron Slick, from Punkin Crick! Hayseed!" Red was about to walk away when the blonde—now prettier than ever—said, "Oh, well.

If he doesn't smoke marijuana." She looked at Red and giggled.

Tony left the girls and hurried to Red's side. "It's all set, pal," he whispered into Red's ear. "She's dying to go out with you. I don't know how you do it, boy, from this distance."

"It's the smell of the silo." Deliberately Red stuck a straw which he had plucked from the upholstery of the car in his mouth. They thought him a bumpkin; he wouldn't disappoint them.

Tony turned and introduced him to the girls who had slowly followed him. "Red, this is *my* girl, Tommy Eden." He turned to the blonde. "This is Bobbie Meredith."

Bobbie extended the whitest hand Red had ever seen. "How do you do?" she said. Her eyes strayed to Red's hair, now slicked down and cowlicked, and she added, "I have to be home early."

Red grabbed her hand and worked it like a pump handle on a dry well. "Sure, ma'am, don't you give that no never mind." He clucked with broad knowingness, which said, "Oh, you kid, and twenty-three-ski-doo."

Tony gave Red a startled look, not sure that Red wasn't pulling their legs. Bobbie grimaced and jerked her hand away from Red. "Brother!" she said, rubbing it. "I bet the cows back in Ogden just loved you!"

"Well, ma'am, I didn't shake their hands." He laughed and slapped his thigh. "That was a zinger, warn't it?" He slapped her on the back so hard she almost fell.

Tony tried to save the situation by hurrying over

and opening the car door for Tommy. Bobbie leaned toward her and whispered, "I may poison him before the night's over."

"I'll toss you for it," said Tommy, getting in.

Bobbie turned to get in the rumble seat and froze. Red already had climbed in. "You might at least help me up," she said icily.

"Plumb forgot my manners, ma'am," Red said. He reached down and grabbed her by both hands and lifted her into the air, depositing her in the seat. He reached over, tapped Tony on the shoulder and said, "Giddyap."

They didn't talk much on the drive to Harlem. Bobbie had a trace of a southern accent and Red guessed she was from the South. "Why yes," she said, "Memphis. How did you know?" He explained that he had talked to many of the young southern musicians who had brought jazz up the river from New Orleans to Memphis, Chicago, westward to San Francisco, and eastward to New York.

Tony used the drive to show off his Stutz, throttling it down to a one-mile-an-hour chug-a-lug in the accepted style of the day. "Listen to her talk," he said, caressing the big wooden steering wheel.

"I been listening," said Red. "That's 'cause she's from Memphis."

The car rolled through darkened streets and turned corners until it came to a brightly lit section, pungent with smells of fried food and jam-packed humanity. Tony tooled the car to a stop and this time Red lifted Bobbie out more gently.

They went down a flight of stairs below the sidewalk

to a plain doorway over which hung a single fly-specked light bulb. Tony rapped on the door, one-two-three, one-two. A peephole opened and a pair of eyes looked out. The door opened and Tony nodded to the doorman as though he had been there many times before.

Before a crowded, smoke-filled room a small dance orchestra played "Jada." On a postage-sized dance floor in front of them men and women, white and black, stomped to a Dixieland tune. Before the Negro headwaiter could show them to their little round table, Red grabbed Bobbie and pushed her toward the floor. He grabbed her around the waist in a bear hug and began stepping on her feet, bumping into other couples.

Bobbie grimaced and darted a look toward her feet. "Say, plowboy—are you sure you've danced before?"

"Yes, ma'am, lots of times."

He shoved against her and Bobbie stumbled. "With girls?"

"When I couldn't get nothin' better." He stepped on her foot again, deliberately.

Bobbie screamed so loud that everyone looked. "I know it may seem like a weird tribal dance, but this is how the dance usually is done." She broke from Red's grip and showed him a proper hold while moving her feet more to the music. "One and two and one and two and one and—"

"I think I got it." Red whirled her gracefully around the floor, laughing to himself.

Bobbie glared at him, realizing she'd been had. "Why you dirty—"

Red's grin was as wide as the land erosions which were becoming scenic national parks back in Utah. "Yes, ma'am!"

Who was this drawling Deep South patootie to call him bumpkin? Why he had been facing the public, entertaining people, all his life. He had even formed his own jazz band at Culver Military Academy, to play at school dances. He liked this dark-eyed blonde and wanted to make a good impression on her. By acting like an oaf now he would look later, by comparison, like the charming, handsome, talented fellow he really was. This was not one of the painted chorus girls about whom his parents had warned him. She might dance to the jazz that his father called the music of free love, because it had come up from the red-light district of New Orleans' infamous Storyville, but this girl was a lady. A southern lady, if you please.

Suddenly, Red felt a pain hit his foot and run up his leg, forcing his eyes closed. It felt as though the roof had fallen on it. He opened his eyes to see Bobbie stamping his toes as hard as she could. Now he laughed. The music stopped and Red led her triumphantly toward Tony and Tommy at the table.

Tony grinned at Bobbie. "I should have warned you," he whispered as she sat down. "The kid is hep."

A waiter came and set teacups on the table. Red sat down looking puzzled. "We didn't order tea," he said. He never drank tea at home, except squaw tea, or "Mormon" tea which his mother brewed from desert herbs, all stimulants being against his religion. The waiter frowned at him. Red looked from Tony to the other girls. "Did they order tea?" he asked.

"Red, this is tea like my mother used to make for Sunday afternoons with the Mafia!" Tony explained. He held a cup up for Red to sniff. "Ninety-proof. It's in teacups in case of a raid."

Red blushed. "Don't you think I know that?"

"No," Bobbie smiled. "Have you ever been in a speakeasy before?"

"Dozens of times," Red said. Not only had he never been in one, he had never heard a prohibition booze den called by that name before. He raised his cup and took a gulp. It felt like he had swallowed a fireplace. He gasped.

Bobbie was watching him curiously. "Oh, we've got a live one here," she laughed. She passed him her cup. "Have some more tea."

"Plowboy, huh?" Red spluttered. "I'll show you, plowboy!" He downed her cup. At that instant the lights in the club were dimmed. "Wood alcohol, I've gone blind!" he screamed. Then he heard Tony saying, "Red, they just turned out the lights."

He coughed his embarrassment. "Don't you think I know that?"

"No," Bobbie said, and if she hadn't been so pretty he could have hated her.

A spotlight shone up on the stage and a cornet sounded. The spotlight grew, revealing the musician, a heavy-set Negro. Tony nudged Red. "They call him 'dipper-mouth,' 'Satchmo,' and 'Kid Louis,'" he said. "He's just about the greatest cornet player I ever heard."

Affected by the whisky and the music, Red did not hear Tony. His temples pounded, his stomach burned and his eyes glazed but he would have known Louis Armstrong in any condition. He had heard him in Chicago en route east and before that, in his room at Culver when he was hiding from the upper class hazers, had listened to recordings by the men who influenced him. Louis had come up to Chicago from Storyville with King Oliver's Creole Jazz Band. Oliver's "Chimes Blues" had been the first recording to feature Louis as the soloist and there was no mistaking the rich full tone, the vibrant life and beauty of his playing. Red had heard Louis with Fletcher Henderson's Band just a few days before, at the Roseland Ballroom in New York, and he had gone to hear him again at every opportunity.

He had even heard the story of how Louis had learned to play in a Negro waifs' home band when he was sent to the home for shooting off a pistol in a New Orleans street during a New Year's celebration. Three or four years later Louis was playing in the bawdy houses of the red-light district, where the charms of the ladies of the evening were advertised in their own *Blue Book,* and later on a Mississippi River excursion boat. His style was more staccato than King Oliver's, who played with a drag. It was filled with rapid, intricate phrasing in high registers. He played full and round F's and G's above high C until the birds couldn't hear. Like Beiderbecke, he blew with his heart.

The music had a hypnotic effect upon Red. Even after the lights came on he sat without moving. Finally Tony nudged him. "Hey, man, how about that bugle?"

Red did not reply. Tony's girl friend reached over and tugged Red's sleeve. "Like it?" she said.

26

"Of course," Red said finally, playing the tune over in his mind. "But my arrangement is better." He took another sip of his "tea" not realizing how his statement had sounded. But he had meant it. If his blowing was not as good, his arrangements were. Jazz should be written, he felt. It could be written, and he could play it *as* written. When he got his band together for the Pelham Heath job the musicians would be permitted individual expression. They would play with freedom, but it would be disciplined freedom, so that the result would have an over-all pattern.

Improvisation was fine, within bounds. Without written restraints, music would become too wild. He didn't know it then, but his mind was stating beliefs that would bring him both fame and calumny; make some musicians call him great, others call him corny. He took another drink of his "tea."

Bobbie caught his eye. "For a minute, I didn't think you were paying attention."

"My arrangement is better—but that's the best cornet I ever heard next to my father's," Red said.

Bobbie looked at him with disbelief. "Let's you drink to that," she said. She picked up another teacup and poured it into Red's. Automatically, he sipped it. He coughed. He poured it into the saucer, blew on it, and drank it while the others laughed.

Armstrong began to sing "Bill Bailey," backed up by the band. Red, carried away by the rhythm, emboldened by this wonderful tea, joined in, singing to himself first, then louder and louder. Armstrong became annoyed. He tried to outshout Red but with no success. Finally he picked up his cornet and blasted at him.

Red stopped singing. "He's changing weapons!" he shouted drunkenly. "Where's my horn?" He reached for his cornet.

Tony grabbed his arm. "Man, don't start that! They'll blow you right out of the room!"

Red pulled loose and started for the dance band.

Louis concluded the number just as Red came stumbling up to the bandstand. Armstrong grabbed Red's arm, supporting him. "What can I do for you?" he said.

"I'm going to show you how to play this thing," Red replied. He began to fit the mouthpiece into the cornet, but had difficulty making ends meet.

"You look a little shaky, son," Louis said. "You'd better sit this one out. We'll get to the volunteers later."

Armstrong had handled drunken planters and plain mean fighting men in the Storyville houses and on the riverboats, and he certainly knew how to handle this country boy.

Red was offended. "You don't think I can play it, huh? Well, I happen to be the second best cornet player in Ogden, Utah!"

"North Ogden, or South Ogden?" Louis spoke loud enough for the audience to hear. Everyone laughed.

Red turned to the audience. "You may not think that's much, but my father lives there and he's the best cornet player in the whole world. Ask anybody!"

Armstrong raised his horn. "Well, boy, if he ain't Gabriel you're in trouble. Play."

Red finally succeeded in getting the mouthpiece in place. He raised his horn, then lowered it again. He looked around for the music stands but saw none. "Where's the arrangement?" he asked.

Armstrong laughed and his band joined him. "Arrangement? Son, nobody writes down Dixieland. You just let it happen."

"Suppose it happens great one time—and you want it to happen again exactly the same way?"

"Can't be done! That'd be like tapping a nightingale on the shoulder, and saying, 'How's that again?'"

Laughter filled the room again. Red reached into his coat pocket and pulled out some music. "Well, I wrote some down. I've been writing it down since I was thirteen." He raised his horn and said, " 'The Battle Hymn of the Republic.' "

Armstrong touched Red's shoulder. "Maybe you'd better come back Sunday. I don't think this prayer meeting is ready for that kind of music."

Red glared at the musicians. "Just try to stay with me," he rasped.

"Don't look back or you'll be trampled to death," Louis said. He raised his cornet, waiting for Red to take the lead. Red tapped his foot for the beat and put his cornet to his lips. The first note was pure, rich and golden. The second note was pure garbage. He tried desperately to get back to the melody but he couldn't make it. He lowered his cornet to its case. "I'm going to be very sick." He pushed his way off the stage to a howl of laughter.

"Excuse it, folks," Armstrong announced. "Somebody must have put alcohol in our liquor." Everyone was convulsed with laughter except Bobbie. She had been watching Red with sympathy and not a little shame. It was all her fault. She had goaded him to drink too much.

While the music played, she followed him to the men's room and waited outside, holding his cornet. After a while Red came out looking pale and wiping his mouth with the back of his hand. He leaned against the wall, limp. Bobbie walked up to him. "Feel better?" she said.

"Where's my horn?" Red said.

Bobbie handed it to him. "You feel better, all right."

Red fondled the horn. "There isn't another like it in the whole world. My father gave it to me." Now he'd blow it for the glory of Professor E. W. Nichols. Master Loring Nichols would entertain on the cornet. These people would applaud just like the people in Ogden and Salt Lake and San Jose and St. George and Cedar City. Red thought of the day the horn was handed to him. His father had received a shipment of instruments and Red had watched him unpack them. His father took out a horn, handed it to the three-year-old boy and said, "Blow, boy." He blew and that was it. His father decided he'd play it. He built a little stand to hold the cornet so that Red wouldn't drop it. He had gone on to be heard by Sousa, to lead parades and to play for his father's women's band. He came out of his reverie. He looked frankly into Bobbie's eyes. "I've got to tell you something," he murmured. "That's the first drink of liquor I ever had in my whole entire life. Since I was born. And I wish I hadn't been."

Bobbie felt a surge of warmth and pity for him. "I'd never have guessed, Red," she said.

"Another thing, nobody in Ogden calls me Red except me. My name is Loring. I was christened 'Ernest Loring Nichols' although the birth certificate people accidentally dropped the 'Ernest.' I couldn't help it."

She touched his forearm. "You're ashamed of all the wrong things. You know what my real name is? Willa. Willa Stutesman. Willa Stutesman."

Red smiled weakly. "Hello, Willa."

"Hello, Loring. Now you just take it easy. I'll get your hat, then you can take me home. Let's not wait for Tony." She held her arm for Red to take.

"You mean you want just me alone to take you home? By myself, without anybody but only me?"

Bobbie nodded. "It doesn't really matter that you'll never be the greatest cornet player in the world."

Red pulled away. "You don't believe me either."

Bobbie sighed. "Oh, please, just wait here, Loring."

He looked defiant. "Call me Red."

She threw him a hopeless glance and started off.

Armstrong's number concluded to raucous applause and whistling.

Red pulled himself to his feet. He yanked his cornet out and spread the music out on a table in front of him. As the noise died down he started to play "The Battle Hymn of the Republic."

A few persons in the audience turned to stare. They did not faze him. He liked attention. Leaning against the wall, tired and sick—but determined—he blew loud and clear. For the moment he was in a church meeting in Ogden. Master Loring Nichols, aged five, entertaining on the cornet. Gradually his playing became a driving, syncopated demonstration of his virtuosity.

Now he had the audience with him. No one spoke. Dishes became quiet. Even the teacups were silent. The musicians picked up the accompaniment, one by one. Finally Armstrong raised his horn and joined in, following Red's lead. Triumphantly, on a wave of sound, Red staggered down toward the bandstand.

Not only did Armstrong play with him, but he sang with him. "Glory, glory, hallelujah, His truth is marching on!"

The applause was deafening, and confusing. Red saw that Armstrong was clapping too. He stepped down from the bandstand, took Bobbie by the arm and started out. Nearing the door, he heard Armstrong say, "Get that boy's license number! He caught the nightingale." A nightingale that makes little bird tracks on lined paper that other birds can follow.

Going home in the taxi Red told Bobbie all about himself. "When I was five years old I was playing 'Carnival in Venice' at church festivals." He looked into her eyes. "You ever been in a Mormon Church festival in Ogden, Utah?" His tongue still was thick from the tea.

"I don't think so."

"It goes like this: 'Mrs. Webster will now sing "The Last Rose of Summer." ' " He sang a couple of bars off key. While singing he saw something in her eyes. He kissed her and found out what it was. "Where was I?" he said, giddy now with emotion as well as from the alcohol.

Bobbie's lips brushed his cheek. "At a church festival. And I shouldn't be with you because my mother says musicians are no good."

Red raised his voice to stentorian tones: "'And now Professor E. W. Nichols and the Nichols family orchestra featuring Master Loring Nichols, aged five, on the silver cornet.'" He nuzzled Bobbie's ears. "Real silver, too. It was my father's. He still has it. A one, a two, a three!" He pretended to play "Carnival in Venice." Then before he knew it he was kissing her. He liked it. "How much longer is the cab ride?" he asked rapturously.

"Oh, it's a long way to Brooklyn."

"Good. You live in Brooklyn?" he said suddenly.

"Yes, and it's so late, I know I'm going to catch it from my mother."

"Well, as long as you're going to catch it, you might as well get kissed again," he said. It was a long kiss. During it, Red thought he heard automobile horns and a policeman's whistle playing Mendelssohn's "Wedding March."

He blinked at Bobbie. "Do you hear that?"

"What?"

"Never mind, you will." He tried to kiss her again but she pushed him away. "I hardly know you," she said. "You're full of tea."

They reached Brooklyn and Red took her to her door. He tried to kiss her again but she jerked away. Safely home, her attitude was changing. "Mr. Nichols," she began stiffly as though about to recite something long rehearsed, "I may dance in the chorus but I'm not the fast girl you apparently think I am. Good night. And don't bother to telephone." With that, she ran into the house.

CHAPTER 3

RED was dumfounded by Bobbie's about face. She had seemed so nice on their blind date. Early the next morning he telephoned her. She refused to talk to him.

It was a great blow. Only a nineteen-year-old could have suffered so intensely—and so briefly. It had been love at first sight—but there were many other sights for a handsome, talented redhead with money in his jeans to see. He dated one chorus girl after another and took them up to Harlem to hear Armstrong and another famous cornettist, called Jabbo, who had just got in from New Orleans. Jabbo was the rage; but in Red's opinion could not touch Louis, Bix or, for that matter, himself.

Still remembering his razor-strop spankings for playing jazz, Red now played it with a vengeance for the wild, fast crowd which drank bathtub gin and danced as though there were no tomorrow. Mornings, after he was through playing for Wil Paradise, Red took his horn around to the after-hours spots and jammed with the hot bands. From the church festival in Ogden he had gone to the ball of Bacchus. All around him, in this exhilarating world of jazz, were rebels like himself, and, in the speakeasies where he played, the gangsters who gave people what the law would not. In this atmosphere people advocated "companionate marriage" in which legalized birth control would be practiced and childless couples could call it quits at any time with impunity.

And Red Nichols was leading his own band. He had quit Paradise, taken over Johnny Johnson's surplus engagement at Pelham Heath Inn, bringing together Joe Venuti, violin; Joe Zeigler, drums; Gerald Finney, piano; Freddie Morrow, saxophone; Dudley Fosdick, melophone, and himself on cornet. The Inn was a speakeasy and Babe Ruth, when he wasn't knocking home runs for the Yankees, was trying to drink it dry. Babe, an early fan of Red's, would get so plastered and be poured out so late that Morrow would bet Venuti he wouldn't get a hit next day, only to lose when Ruth would get two walks and a homer out of four times up. Impressed by this, Red started consuming quite a lot of alcohol himself, feeling that a man had to drink to look and sound like a jazz artist. He quickly learned that nobody can play stoned.

He bought a raccoon coat but had to sell it when the Pelham engagement ended. After that he played briefly with a number of bands, including the California Ramblers. About that time Bix Beiderbecke came to New York with the famous Wolverines to play at the Cinderella Ballroom. Red lived at the Pasadena Hotel and proudly drove a Jewett, about which the ads said, "Try to pass it on a hill." Red had a piano in his room and Bix frequently came and stayed with him, bringing in his suitcase nothing more than a pair of dirty underwear and an old tie, some socks and a handkerchief or two, and his cornet in a paper sack.

He and Red would sit around playing records and drinking, or Bix would sit at the piano for hours, playing things like Eastwood Lane's "Adirondack Sketches." Bix was an unhappy, lonely guy. He'd leave Red's place for a week or ten days at a time and return shattered from drink and loss of sleep. Because Red admired Bix's cornet and had copied some of his phrasing, he tried to get Bix to play it but Bix seldom would do it, preferring to sit improvising on the piano. When he did blow his horn, Red chimed in on his, and some of the world's greatest cornet duets were performed but, being unrecorded, were to be lost to posterity. When Bix left the Wolverines, Red was offered his place in the band. He turned it down, despite the fact that he idolized the band's style, because it could not pay enough to please him. It took a lot of money to entertain chorus girls in speakeasies, and Red blew it out of his horn of plenty, playing for the Ramblers, for Joe Candullo, Willie Creager, Lou Gold, Ross Gorman, Cass Hagan, Sam Lannin and many others.

By 1925 "flaming youth" was really ablaze and Red Nichols was its flaming-haired symbol. F. Scott Fitzgerald was its patron saint; Mencken, its spokesman; "Jelly Roll" Morton, its musical egoist; Gershwin, its discovery; Jimmy Walker, its song-writing mayor; Irving Berlin, Gus Kahn, Cliff Friend, Irving Caesar, Buddy de Sylva, its songwriters.

Flaming youth sang "Yes, Sir, That's My Baby," "Who Takes Care of the Caretaker's Daughter While the Caretaker's Busy Taking Care?," "Ukulele Lady," "Then I'll Be Happy" and, drunk on bad booze, "Show Me the Way to Go Home."

Falsetto tenors trilled "Sleepy Time Gal," "Song of the Vagabonds," "Song of the Flame," "Moonlight and Roses," "Just a Cottage Small by a Waterfall," "If You Were the Only Girl in the World," "If You Knew Susie, Like I Know Susie," "Down by the Winegar Woiks," "Drifting and Dreaming," "Five Foot Two Eyes of Blue," "The Hills of Home," "I'm Sitting on Top of the World," "Cecilia," "Brown Eyes, Why Are You Blue?," "Always," "Don't Bring Lulu" and "Collegiate."

Women's suffrage had succeeded so well that Nellie Tayloe Ross had been elected Governor of Wyoming, the first woman to hold such an office. Miriam ("Ma") Ferguson was installed Governor of Texas and men tried going to jail rather than pay alimony. Down in Dayton, Tennessee, they were having a trial to ascertain, in effect, whether man came from a monkey and Thomas Scopes was found guilty of teaching this. Flesh-colored silk stockings became the rage, replacing black ones. There was an earthquake in Santa Barbara, California, and a land boom in Florida and California. *The Jazz Singer*, *The Green Hat*, *Craig's Wife*, George White's *Scandals* and Earl Carroll's *Vanities* were running on Broadway, and motion pictures included *The Big Parade*, *The Merry Widow*, *The Phantom of the Opera* and *The Son of the Sheik*. Red

Grange was a football star at the University of Illinois. And Red Nichols was beginning to catch on. Also, he was in love.

Her name was Hannah Williams. She was sixteen years old and a beautiful dream who sang with her sister, Dorothy, in George White's *Scandals*. Red dated her as often as a long line of suitors would allow. He coached her in her singing by running over her numbers with his cornet, having her follow him note for note, tone for tone. Red begged her to marry him but she put him off. Shortly afterward, Red's roommate, an actor, went to Chicago to work with the Marx Brothers. Later, Hannah went there to work, too. The next thing Red knew, she and his roommate were married.

Red's heart was broken. He drank a little whisky, played a blues on his horn and had himself a cry or two. It hurt for quite a while. Then he met Bobbie again at a party. She was more beautiful than he remembered and brunette now. After chasing her for a week she finally consented to give him a date. They began going steady.

He was in love again. For keeps.

Meantime, he started making recordings for the California Ramblers, the Hottentots, the Louisiana Rhythm Kings, Miff Mole's Molers, Red & Miff Stompers, the Charleston Chasers, the Redheads and the Cotton Pickers. Life became one recording session after another and could not have been dizzier if he had stood on the turntable and turned with it. He estimated he blew enough air through his cornet to fill the zeppelins then sailing the skies.

He recorded Hoagy Carmichael's "Boneyard Shuffle," and made "Ida, Sweet as Apple Cider" because Bobbie had asked him to play something "sweet." It sold over a million records. His first composition, "Nervous Charlie," he recorded for Pathé Actuelle with the band going under the name of "The Redheads." If a tune was any good he recorded it—"Feelin' No Pain," "Bugle Call Rag," "Alabama Stomp," "Eccentric," "Nobody's Sweetheart," "Avalon," "Rose of Washington Square," "Indiana," "Dinah," "China Boy," "After You've Gone," "Clarinet Marmalade," "Cornfed," "Hallelujah," "How Come You Do Me Like You Do?," "I've Got Rhythm," "I'm Just Wild About Harry," "Margie," "Japanese Sandman," "My Sweetie Went Away," "Peanut Vendor," "Roses of Picardy," "The Sheik," "Sweet Georgia Brown," "Sweet Sue," "Tea for Two," "They Didn't Believe Me" and "Washboard Blues."

While Armstrong was switching to the mellower trumpet, Red stayed with the cornet, claiming it was a better solo instrument. He had so many recording dates that he could put men on salary, just to make records. In those days jazz musicians made records as much to impress other musicians as to sell them. Every record became an experiment and every man awaited the next man's records as avidly as the scientist awaits the results of another's experiments in his own field.

Red filled in in radio orchestras, but never took these seriously, feeling that radio was a passing fad.

In December, 1926, he began a three-year-long series of recordings for Brunswick under the name of Red Nichols and His Five Pennies, suggested by his drummer Vic Berton. Sometimes the Five Pennies grew to six, eight and ten men and frequently included Jimmy Dorsey, Eddie Lang, Miff Mole, Joe Venuti, Arthur Schutt, Berton, Benny Goodman, Lennie Hayton and Fud Livingston. Glenn Miller often filled in as trombonist and arranger. One of the first tunes recorded by the Pennies was "That's No Bargain," written by Nichols himself. On that record Nichols played cornet; Dorsey, clarinet and alto sax; Artie Schutt, piano; Eddie Lang, guitar, and Vic Berton, drums.

While the critics said Nichols imitated Beiderbecke, sometimes note by note but without catching the subtlety of Bix's style, they acknowledged Red was doing much more for jazz by bringing hot musicians to recordings. They agreed that Nichols was a better technician but that Beiderbecke felt the music more. Althought Beiderbecke lacked a satisfactory command of his instrument, he came nearer than any other to being the ideal jazz musician. He had punch, and a sense of attack and phrasing that few have achieved. Whereas Beiderbecke did not read music well, often playing by ear, Red was a purist, who strove to write down everything and to eliminate the harsh strident tones of some of the early jazz. Yet, like Bix, he had a sense of harmonic structure that enabled him to take off, out of any chord sequence.

But he was too successful to care what the critics said. When he found time to reply to charges that he copied Beiderbecke, he admitted it readily. "Bix is great," he said. "I have no compunctions against taking what I like. There isn't a musician alive who isn't influenced by someone. Plenty of players are influenced by Louis Armstrong—and many by me, including Beiderbecke, who copied my 'false fingering' to give various colors or timbre to a note without changing the note itself. Armstrong was influenced by Joe Oliver, his sponsor. So what?"

So this: He was in such demand that frequently he found his recording dates conflicting and had to send out other trumpet and cornet players to substitute for him. Many of them came to prominence this way; among the trumpet players, Leo McConville and Manny Klein.

Paul Whiteman, who had Bing Crosby and the Rhythm Boys with him, wanted Red. In order to get him, he agreed to take all the Pennies. Everybody signed their contracts with Whiteman except Red's favorite, his idol, the great trombonist Miff Mole. Miff's reneging made Red unhappy and he told Whiteman. Whiteman agreed to let Red out shortly, which he did.

Meantime, Bobbie was dancing in another Earl Carroll's *Vanities*. So was Hannah Williams, her marriage having been annulled after only a few days. Watching them both on stage one night, Red got that old feeling again. He signaled Hannah to meet him after the show. Bobbie intercepted the signal. She met him, too. "Make up your mind—me or her," Bobbie said. Red made up his mind fast. Bobbie.

They were married at City Hall. Whiteman was their best man. Red had so many play engagements that day that Whiteman had to take the bride home for him. A few hours later Red and Bing Crosby, en route to another play date, stuck their heads in the bridal suite to say "hello." At 3 a.m. Bobbie, tired of waiting for her bridegroom, drove home to Brooklyn and mother in his automobile. She left the emergency brake handle on and the brakes burned on that drive. She was burned too . . . by the hours musicians kept. There would be some changes made.

CHAPTER 4

Bobbie would be good for him. She was a homebody who knew how to cook, sew and knit—an old-fashioned southern lady who danced *in* the chorus, but not *with* it. And everybody said it was a good match because Red, while dancing *around* the primrose path, had not danced *down* it. In fact, they said, a lot of bachelor musicians soon were to find out that mama don' 'low no reefer smokin', and if they came to her house smelling of the acrid, sickening smoke, Bobbie would make them air their clothes out first.

Bobbie had quit her job the day before the marriage ceremony, wanting to make a home for them, but Red wanted her to try singing with a band, to be near him. He had a commitment to play a short time again for Wil Paradise and having become a bigger man, had forced Paradise to take Bobbie, too. As a matter of fact, he condescended to sign again with Paradise mainly because he hated Paradise's honeyed style so much that he wanted to blow with Wil's boys again to let them all see how he had gone up in the world and to let them hear some real music for a change.

But the engagement was contracted to start on the second night of their marriage. Having spent the first night apart, they were in no mood for it. Besides, friends were giving them a reception that night. They reported for work only a few minutes before the band was to start playing for the evening, making Paradise angry that they hadn't come for rehearsal. He turned a deaf ear to Red's request for a couple of days' postponement of their contract. He was acutely aware of Red's condescending attitude toward him and resented having Bobbie forced on him. "Look, hot shot," he began snidely, "you get five-minute breaks, don't you? That's two choruses and a reprise. That's all the time you get off here."

Red asked about some jazz arrangements he had sent to Paradise.

"They're in the ash can," Wil snarled. "I will not be put out of business with that broken-down Dixieland. Play it in your bawdy houses and coming home from colored funerals, but not for me. I gave that tone-deaf broad of yours a job—what else do you want?"

The lights started to dim. "Now sit down and blow." Wil rapped on his music stand. Red reluctantly seated himself and they started to play. He squirmed through Wil's greeting to the audience: "Hello, one and all. A fond welcome to the sweetest music ever played. We're all a little misty-eyed tonight, because our own Loring Red Nichols, the finest cornet in the country, has returned to us—with a bride—none other than the new addition to our happy family—our society chanteuse, the lovely Miss Bobbie Meredith."

There was polite applause. Wil motioned to Red and Bobbie to get up and they did so and took a bow. Wil thought they stood too long and hastily motioned them down. To the audience, he said, "To the loving couple, we dedicate our theme with our blessings."

He picked up his megaphone and began to croon and whistle "Paradise." . . . "And when she holds my hand, la da da da, da da dah, dah. Then I will understand, da da da dah, da da da dah. One kiss, da da, da dah, da dum da dah, dum da da dah, to Paradise."

Red listened, burning. "Misty-eyed. I'll make him misty-eyed," he muttered.

Bobbie looked straight ahead and addressed Red out of the corner of her mouth. "Don't do anything crazy. You'll get into trouble with the union."

Wil concluded his saccharine chorus. As he turned he threw Bobbie and Red a kiss. That did it. As Wil picked up his baton to conduct the rest of the number, Red got to his feet before Bobbie could stop him and grabbed Wil's megaphone. Wil turned, startled, but in front of all the dancers he was helpless. Red lifted the megaphone and started to croon and whistle "Paradise." It was a devastating take-off on Wil Paradise and every other thin-voiced crooner strong enough to lift a megaphone. It was the Scotch-Irish devil in Red coming out and he couldn't help it. In other days he had walked off the bandstand during numbers he didn't like. He had deserted his father's ladies' band by running down an alley, humiliated by the taunts of playmates. He had heeded the siren call from New Orleans. There was no other music and he had to say what he thought of Wil Paradise's sickly sweet style in unmistakable terms, by showing him how he sounded.

The band doubled over with laughter, hardly able to play. The dancers enjoyed it. Wil Paradise kept a straight face, his teeth clenched.

All the rest of the evening Wil glared at Red. At every opportunity he criticized his playing. He said, "I'll want to see you later."

Red sent Bobbie on home to dress for the wedding reception, knowing what was coming. After the last set of the evening, Paradise turned to Red, an evil glint in his eye. Red rose to his feet just as Wil opened his mouth. Red's right fist shot out, clipping Wil's loose chin. The resulting free impact of jaw bone against temple knocked Wil cold.

Wil was unable to attend the reception. No one mentioned the fight to Bobbie but she suspected something irregular by the way Paradise's sidemen, drinking freely of champagne, kept toasting Red, alone.

Later, when they had gone to their hotel suite, Bobbie asked Red if he had apologized to Wil, as she had asked him to do.

"We had a talk after the show," Red hedged.

"Well?"

Red looked at his hands, newly fascinated by his shortened right forefinger which he had stuck in a lawnmower as a child, but which had not impaired his lightning valve work on the cornet. "You wouldn't want me to stay in the band if I wasn't happy, would you?" he said. "Can you imagine another couple of months of 'Hello, everyone, I'm a little misty-eyed tonight'?"

Bobbie moved away from him to unpack their bags. "Oh, Loring—you didn't even try."

Red followed her. "I did try. I tried my best, but he just wouldn't listen to reason, so I hit him in the mouth and quit."

"But we just got married!" She turned to him, relaxing momentarily. "Well, at least, *I* have a job. Even if I *can't* sing." She kissed him.

Red held her. "I'd better tell you now. I hit him for both of us."

Bobbie pulled away from him. "You what?" She turned and ran from the bedroom into the living room. Red ran after her. "I couldn't have my wife working for a guy like that. You didn't want the job anyway. Someday he'll be working for me."

"It's not the job," Bobbie said. "It's your rashness. You'll get a bad reputation." She studied him. "I don't even know you. You're a stranger. My mother was right. She said you're unstable; you do crazy things all the time."

"Let's talk about that tomorrow," Red said. "This is our wedding night. Pardon. Second night. Or do we count the first?"

"It was a mistake," Bobbie went on. "It was all a horrible mistake!" She ran back to the bedroom and slammed the door.

Red crossed to the door and called her. He tried the

door knob. She had locked it. He rattled it. "What kind of a bridal suite is this?" he asked. "The door's locked!"

Bobbie's voice came back full of determination. "You can sleep out there on the couch. We'll both get a good night's rest."

"I don't want a night's rest."

Bobbie opened the door and handed him his pajamas and toothbrush. Red saw a chance to make peace. "I'll go back and beg Wil for that job. I'll play so soft nobody will hear me."

Bobbie gave a scornful laugh. "I doubt it. You know why you quit Wil? Because he didn't like your arrangements. Isn't that true?" She handed him a blanket and pillow she had taken off the bed.

Red took them without looking. "What if it is?"

"You're thinking only of your music. If you don't think of me first on our wedding night, or the second night, what chance would I have on an anniversary?" She pulled her hand free and closed the door again.

Red went to the couch and began to undress. After a bit Bobbie knocked on the door. "I forgot to give you the toothpaste," she called.

Red was reconciled to spending his honeymoon alone. He started making up his couch. "Squeeze it under the door," he said.

Bobbie opened the door. "Here it is."

Red crossed to her. "Hello," he said.

She handed him the toothpaste and closed the door again. Red tossed it aside and started to turn out the lights.

Bobbie called to him, "Good night." He didn't reply and, after a pause, she said, "I've never slept in a bridal suite before."

"Neither have I," said Red.

"Loring, how much did this suite cost you?"

"Will you stop that?"

"I want to know."

"Fifty bucks, but it's all right. We're using both rooms."

"Fifty dollars, what a crazy thing to do!"

Red sat on the edge of the couch and reached for an apple in a gift basket on an end table. He took a bite. "I wanted you to have the best," he mumbled. "A wedding night is something you want to remember for the rest of your life." He swallowed. "I'll remember *this* one after I'm dead. Last night, too."

Her tone was more conciliatory. "But so much money!"

"I'm crazy," Red said. "Ask your mother." He took another bite from his apple, and chewed it thoughtfully.

After a moment the door opened and Bobbie came out. She was in her negligee. She walked toward him, a gossamer dream. She sat down on the couch beside him. "It's a lovely suite," she said tentatively.

"Have an apple," Red said. "The manager sent this up. Free."

"Thanks," Bobbie said, taking the apple and biting into it. She tucked her feet up under her. "You'll make a terrible husband," she said coyly. "I'll never know from one minute to the next what you're going to do."

49

"That's all right. Neither will I."

She kissed him. "Are you really a Mormon, like you said?" she asked.

He nodded.

She kissed him again. "Just don't practice any Mormonism around here, Mister."

"What do you mean?"

"Just one wife."

He laughed at this common misconception of his religion. "I haven't had one wife yet," he said.

But that was only a matter of time.

CHAPTER 5

RED NICHOLS and his Five Pennies were almost an instant hit with jazz fans. As their records rolled out from New York to be played on crank-up phonographs, demands for the band to appear at big college dances came in from all over the East. Intermittently Red put together "pick-up" bands and traveled far, fast and wide, cashing in on this popularity.

Like his father before him who cracked his knuckles when he hit clinkers, he became a martinet and a perfectionist. After discovering that whisky positively did not improve jazz music but only made bad notes more tolerable, he became, with Bobbie's help and blessing, a temperate artist who demanded sobriety and tidiness of his musicians. On the bandstand he kept a "mistake kitty" which the boys hated. If one made a mistake and tried to hide it with a complicated run of pretty, lacy embroidery around the clinker, Red fined him twenty-five cents. The money was kept in the kitty to be passed out twenty-five cents at a time to the men whenever they made mistakes and acknowledged them and indicated they would try to do better next time.

Good musicians looked up to him. George Gershwin complimented his approach to jazz. Hoagy Carmichael, a struggling song-writer whose "Boneyard Shuffle" Red had recorded, wrote to him asking advice on whether to continue his law studies or come to Tin Pan Alley and write music. Red told him to come.

Musicians who could create on their instruments got the opportunity to show what they could do. He permitted this for two reasons. He could buy abbreviated arrangements containing big blank ad lib sections much cheaper than complete arrangements, and he also felt that *regulated* ad libbing was necessary to the heart of jazz. Yet he never would permit musicians to stray completely away from the paper. In ordering an arrangement written, he'd say where he wanted a jazz chorus, where a modulation, where a change of key and where each musician would do his ad lib solo. In that way he tried to satisfy the musician's creative urges while satisfying his own demands that music have a theme and a format and an understandable melodic line and not be just a meaningless exercise. In this he got much opposition from the stream-of-consciousness crowd which thought everything in jazz should be ad libbed. He steadfastly refused to give quarter. Some musicians, he knew, were bound to hate him for it, to try to count him out as a jazz musician, even call him corny. Yet he had the ability to make men *feel* music as he felt it and he managed to make the music reflect his taste. If a musician couldn't hew to Red's melodic line he was in trouble. Not only was Red the man to see about playing in recording sessions but he was a power in radio, having been hired to serve as a talent contractor for CBS. Whereas earlier he had clowned through his radio dates, now he was succumbing to the medium, taking the good money where it was found.

He had nearly all the good jazz musicians sewed up. At CBS he had Artie Schutt, Miff Mole, Leo McConville and Vic Berton. For plays and recordings he could produce Fud Livingston, Manny Klein, Joe Venuti, Eddie Lang and Chauncey Morehouse.

Music was becoming a "business" with him. He didn't play his horn around the house, feeling he would be as wrong in bringing it home as a shoemaker would in bringing home his work. Bobbie endorsed this because, if jam sessions were not held in her home, rowdies wouldn't break her nice new furniture, leave glass rings on her beloved concert piano, and smell up the drapes with the sickly sweet odor of marijuana. Yet Red often insisted that she travel with him to keep him company. It was on one of the band's junkets to Cornell, University of Maine, Amherst and Princeton that Red learned he was to become a father—an event which ultimately was to change his life, completely and nigh tragically.

He had finished a cornet solo and had left the band to its own devices to dance with Bobbie. She was in that radiant glow of health that frequently comes with pregnancy and the boys in the band, long suspecting her condition, had been making a lottery on when the baby would be born. Jimmy Dorsey was giving odds that she was in her second month; Dave Tough wanted to bet five dollars she was in her third but Tony

Valani wouldn't buy a chance, saying all the good months had been taken. Bobbie had been hesitant about telling Red because she was afraid of how he would react, he was so busy with his career and so insistent on having her travel with the band.

From the bandstand Tony and Dorsey watched Red and Bobbie dancing the Charleston. "He better take it easy," Tony said, "or you'll lose the pool."

Dorsey shushed him. "I don't think she's told him yet," he said, peering intently at them.

Red finished a vigorous routine and pulled Bobbie to him. "You know," he said, "you're the prettiest girl at the prom?"

"Me? I'm an old married lady," Bobbie replied, pleased.

"Never. We've got it whipped. We've got one of those, what do you call it?—companionate marriages. Carefree, gay, and legal."

Bobbie tensed. With him talking like that she couldn't tell him. She snuggled to his shoulder, fighting her fears. "It's been wonderful," she murmured.

"You know something?" Red went on. "The way the band's going, in a couple of years we can stop traveling and have a real, corny, old-fashioned family."

"You mean it?"

"Absolutely," Red said. "A corny little golden-haired girl and a corny little redheaded boy." He whirled her around again, and started into the Black Bottom.

"Red." She began slowly, raising her voice above the din. "I went to a doctor the other day. He has a rabbit that says I'm three months corny."

Red stopped in the middle of a step. "He said what?"

"Do you mind?" Bobbie said. "I mean, a rabbit knowing all about us?"

He quit dancing so hard and embraced her. "No, it's wonderful, it's great. If it has to be, it's great!" He slowed down to half-time, looking alarmed. "Should you be dancing like this? Slow down. Shouldn't you be drinking mineral oil or something? Maybe you ought to lie down?"

Bobbie was beaming. "I feel fine."

"How can *you* feel fine? I'm woozy, my*self*. I'd better get you off the floor."

At that moment, a college boy tried to cut in. Before Red could stop him, Bobbie danced away with him. Red chased after them. "Wait, wait," he yelled at the youth. "Let her go. Let her go." He reached Bobbie and tapped her on the shoulder. "Tell him about the rabbit."

Bobbie just laughed. Red reached out and picked her up in his arms and carried her off the floor.

Bobbie presented Red with a brown-eyed, redheaded baby daughter. A nurse let him hold Dorothy, and he saw the baby looked like him. A moment later he was permitted in to see Bobbie. "Did you see the baby?" she asked weakly.

"Yes," Red said, "but I still love you."

He leaned down and kissed her. Then he handed her a package he had brought with him. "Everything's going to be fine. I'll find an apartment for us in Brooklyn."

Bobbie started opening the package. "Brooklyn, what for?"

"To raise our daughter. That's the best climate for daughters."

"What about fathers?" Bobbie asked.

"I'm canceling the tour. There's plenty of work around New York."

Bobbie wouldn't hear of it. "Not while you're doing so well. What about the boys in the band?"

"Don't worry about them," Red said, "they can all get other jobs."

"But you're supposed to open in Pittsburgh Friday."

"It's time I settled down," Red said. He meant it. His little red-haired girl was the most wonderful thing that had ever happened to him. She was more important than jazz, more important than money. "I'm not opening in Pittsburgh. I'm opening right here. Red Nichols and his One Penny."

Bobbie had finished opening the package and Red reached for it and lifted out a toy rabbit. He held it up, grinning. "I caught him and had him stuffed. That'll teach him to shoot his mouth off."

Bobbie watched him closely. His grin and easy patter didn't fool her. She took the rabbit and set it on the bedtable. "No, Loring. I'm not going to let the baby change our lives. This is something you've wanted so long and worked so hard for. When the baby is strong enough we'll join you on that bus. You can't afford to give up the band now. You've got another mouth to feed."

Red tried to joke away her argument. "I thought *you* were going to feed it."

"I am. And I'll be very happy doing it. And I want you to do what you'll be happy doing." She knew that Red had been unhappy with the radio jobs that he had taken just for the money and she knew he wanted to record and travel with the band.

"Deep down, Loring, what do you really want to do?"

He looked away for a moment and then their eyes met in understanding. Said he, "Have I told you how wonderful you are?"

"Not lately."

The baby was to change Red's life more than he could have imagined.

It began the day he was to bring Bobby and Dorothy home from the hospital. He had bought a big, black Buick sedan as a home-coming gift to Bobbie and had spent the day driving around town picking up things for the baby—crib, bottles, sterilizer, diapers, etc. Being in a celebrating frame of mind, he alternated the stops for the baby's things with stops for a quick shot or two with the boys. By nightfall, both Red and the Buick had taken on a load. Sailing down Fifth Ave., he collided with the rear end of a cab. An argument ensued and the cab driver, seeing that Red was drunk, took his keys and held him until the police arrived.

He spent his first night in jail, at the 47th Street Police Station.

"But I was in good company there," he told Bobbie later. "There was a movie star, a politician, and a college professor in the same cell block."

Traveling around the country with the baby was

ridiculous and ludicrous. Many was the time when the boys in the band were sleeping soundly along the road somewhere that Dorothy would awaken them, crying.

"Here we go again," Jimmy Dorsey would grunt. And Tony would yawn and say, "Hey, somebody give that kid a mute."

Unusual Red Nichols had to have an unusual child. One night when Dorothy awakened on a long haul Red started playing a lullaby he had written as loud as he could blow. The rest of the boys, unable to sleep, joined in. Bobbie yelled for them to stop. "How do you expect Dorothy to go to sleep with *that?*"

"But it's a lullaby I wrote," Red said.

"You know it's a lullaby. I know it's a lullaby. But the baby doesn't. Don't play it like 'The Anvil Chorus.'"

Red turned to the boys. "Pianissimo and andante," he said. "In case any of you have studied music."

They played again, softly, but the baby only cried louder. Outraged, Red gave up. He started to sing as loud as he could. Dorothy, unusual child, went fast asleep.

The band traveled and cut records, established records and won critics' awards.

Anyone who's ever traveled with a baby knows the problems of warming bottles and fixing cereals in hotel rooms. Red's problems were no different, except that Dorothy, at three, preferred Coca Cola and beer to milk and when she was four was just as happy with salami as she was with oatmeal.

They traveled up and down and across the country. Once Red made a triumphant home-coming to Ogden, en route to Los Angeles to play at Fatty Arbuckle's Club. He had a reunion with his stepmother, father and sisters, paid a call on the mayor, shot pool in the poolroom from which his father used to pull him to practice—not just cornet but violin and piano, too—and let it slip out to interviewing reporters that he might make $100,000 that year and had "accidentally" been present at a party where a showgirl allegedly bathed in champagne and which resulted in the perjury conviction of Earl Carroll.

Actually, it was no accident that he was at that party. He had played in the pit for Carroll's *Vanities* and knew the showman well enough to be considered an important guest at any party. His red hair, his wit, his ready smile and his talent—especially his talent—had made him a popular figure with other celebrities drawn to his hot silver horn.

Once, when they went to San Francisco, Bobbie was at her wits' end, trying to take proper care of the little girl on the road. Dorothy insisted on staying up as late as the musicians, which usually was about the hour normal children get up mornings. One night Bobbie came into the hotel room and found Red and the band rehearsing; Dorothy rehearsing with them, singing a song. "What's this?" she demanded.

"Well, I had a great idea," Red said enthusiastically. Wasn't Dorothy cute and precocious and talented? "For the early show, that is, Dorothy and I—" Red went on. He saw Bobbie's sour look. "I think it's a terrible idea, what do you think?" He took a step backward as a precaution.

Dorothy reached for a bottle of beer sitting on the

bass drum and sniffed it. Bobbie quickly reached out and took it away from her. "I think it would be a good idea to get this young lady off the road," Bobbie said.

Red saw Dorothy's disappointment and picked her up and carried her off to their suite and put her to bed. Red was disappointed, too. His father had started his musical education at three. Why couldn't he do the same for his little redhead? She'd knock 'em dead just as Master Loring had, traveling in a covered wagon with his performing bear father. She'd have her name in lights, too. But wouldn't she likely leave home to achieve that, as he had? Threaten to run away, as he had? Start smoking and drinking and traveling with the fast crowd. Red suddenly understood Bobbie's objections. This certainly was not a life for his little girl. But Dorothy's habits were hard to change.

There in San Francisco, Bobbie had to leave Dorothy with Red while she went to Las Vegas to the wedding of a girl friend. Red promised that he would get her to bed early. He did, then asked his boys—Tony Valani, Jimmy Dorsey, Glenn Miller, Dave Tough, Arthur Schutt, and two stray musicians to come up and play poker.

The party was to celebrate Tony's feat in signing the band for a solid ten months on the road at increased prices. "I should have made you manager long ago," Red told him as the game began. "You never could play that guitar, but you handle those bookers like they were blondes."

"One of them is," Tony said. They played for a couple of hours, Miller winning most of the pots, and discussed taking on a couple of sidemen to make their bookers think they were getting their money's worth. They decided on Artie Shaw and a less-known man who played alto sax.

Miller interrupted the business discussion to throw down four aces and there was a groan from the others.

Jimmy Dorsey snarled. "Glenn Miller, boy card shark."

Tough suggested breaking up the game. Schutt agreed. "Yeah, why don't we go down and catch Louis?" he asked.

Red was for playing some more. He had to stay home and baby sit, having given the maid the night off. "The game's just getting started," he countered.

"Spoken like a loser," said Tony, getting up from his chair.

Just then the bedroom door opened and Dorothy appeared in her nightgown. She said, "Daddy, I can't sleep. Hi, fellows."

The boys greeted her fondly.

Red fixed Dorothy with a stern stare. "What are you doing up at two in the morning?"

"Where's Mommy?" Dorothy whined.

"I told you. She's out of town. And if she knew you were still up she'd shoot me. Go to bed."

Tony started for the door. "Come on, Red, the club's just down the street."

Schutt said, "Can't you break away?"

Dorothy looked primly at the piano player. "Mother would shoot him." She crossed to the table and picked up some cards.

"Hey!" Red screamed at her. "You go to bed. You're

getting on my nerves. And put down those cards." He jumped toward her and pulled the cards out of her hands. Dorothy slowly turned away, crying.

Red turned to the card players. "Come on, guys, just one more round."

Tony listened a moment to Dorothy's sobs, shaking his head. He looked accusingly at Red. "Murderer," he said, and left. The others followed.

When they were gone Red crossed to the bedroom. He found Dorothy lying face down on her pillow. He told her he was sorry. She didn't answer. He told her he knew she was lonesome for her mommy. He sat down on the bed. He turned her over. "Come on, aren't we pals? Blood brothers of the Black Foot, Mohawk, Iroquois, Hiawatha Tribe? Ala Kazam, Kazam?"

He gave an Indian call and took her hand in a complicated handshake as he had done many times before to amuse her or give in to her. "Whither thou goest, I goest . . . 'till death do us part?"

"I don't know," she said, as though giving the matter vast thought.

"Oh, come on. How about giving me the last dance, and then to bed?" He lifted her to her feet and very solemnly twirled her to steps they had done many times before. Red bowed. She curtsied, and Red knew he had won. "Good night," he said, picking her up and putting her in the bed. He turned off the light and tiptoed out, closing the door.

No sooner did he get to the living room than Dorothy appeared at the door again.

"I can play poker," she announced importantly.

"I thought you were asleep," Red snapped.

"You've been humming," she said, and pattered over to him.

"Please, Blood Brother," he pleaded. "Sleep."

"Mister Miller taught me," she went on as though she hadn't heard him. "Can't I play?"

"No. Get back in bed this minute."

She turned away crestfallen.

Red got to his feet and looked after her. "Are you crying again?"

"No. Murderer!" she said.

The band spoiled the kid when he didn't. "Okay," he said. "One hand."

Dorothy leaped toward him, grinning gratefully. Red picked her up and deposited her in a chair before the table. He handed her the cards. "But if I beat you," he said, "will you go to bed?"

"Yes, if you win I'll go right to sleep." She spoke confidently as though his winning were only a remote possibility. She sat down and shuffled the cards with surprising and efficient dexterity. "How much are we playing for?" she asked.

"What?"

"Mister Miller says you should always find out first."

Red swallowed his grin. "What are your usual stakes?"

"Peanuts." She indicated a dish of peanuts on the table.

Red took them and divided them, handing half to her and half to himself. "Okay?" he asked.

Dorothy took them. "I won't even count them," she said magnanimously.

63

"Thanks," Red said. He started to deal. Dorothy stopped him and cut the cards. Red looked at her in amazement. Was he rearing a gambler, a monster? Not yet five years old, Dorothy didn't play jacks like other kids; she played jacks or better.

"You can't count," he challenged, probing.

"I can, too! One-two-three-four-five-six-seven-eight-nine-ten-jack-queen-king-ace."

Red's head jerked back. "Did—he—by any chance—teach you to count to—twenty-one?"

"What's that?"

"Shut up and look at your cards."

Dorothy picked up her cards and looked at them. She looked Red in the eye. Tentatively she reached out and put five peanuts in the pot. Red eyed her appraisingly. She wore a poker face. He counted out five peanuts to match hers. He picked up the deck. "How many?" he asked.

Dorothy shook her head, grinning as wide as the Golden Gate. Red couldn't understand why he felt angry at this little dreamboat, but he did. He took two cards.

They looked at one another for a long time. Then Dorothy shoved in all her peanuts. Red tapped his foot, bit his fingernails and mussed his hair. Dorothy hummed a little tune softly, triumphantly. Red tossed in his cards.

"Does that mean I win?" Now she clapped her hands in glee, a child again.

"As though you don't know!" Red snarled.

"Oh, goody." She showed him her cards. "I didn't

have anything. That's called bluffing!" She raked in the peanuts.

"Really?" Red said. He got to his feet and scooped her up, and took her off to bed.

She wouldn't go to sleep. "You didn't win," she said. He spoke crossly to her. She cried. Although her sobs sounded faked, Red couldn't stand it. He sang her a lullaby.

"That's more than a lot of hot-shot composers ever did for their kids," he said, tucking her in.

"I'm not sleepy." Her tone was more threatening than informative.

"Okay, come on. We'll get dressed and go for a walk," Red said, resigned.

"Oh, goody. Will they let me in?"

"Where?"

"Where Uncle Louis is playing." She shrank from Red's stern look. "I won't tell Mother."

"Neither will I."

They grinned at one another in huge understanding.

"Daddy? Are we blood brothers?"

Red nodded. "Whither thou goest..."

" 'Til death do us part?"

"It wouldn't dare!" He bent down and kissed her and gave her the handshake.

Said Dorothy, "Ala Kazam, Kazam."

He dressed her and they went out.

Red had been playing at the Mark Hopkins Hotel and folding up at midnight. Armstrong was playing at a waterfront joint that jumped all night.

Dorothy was as big a hit at the little club as Armstrong was. And a greater novelty. Patrons lavished her with attention. Before long she was sitting on the bandstand with Red and Louis singing a lullaby.

Red looked at his watch. It was three o'clock. He was not being a proper father. "Come on," he ordered Dorothy. "We've got to get back to the hotel. Your mother will skin me alive."

He started to lead her away, but the audience, somewhere beyond the blue haze, applauded the child. Besides, Dorothy was in no mood to go. "I want to hear Mr. Armstrong sing some more."

Louis gave her one of his best, big-eyed, lip-curling looks. "I don't know about you, honey, but I got to get my beauty sleep or I'm a mess in the morning."

Dorothy was adamant. She wanted Louis to play "When the Saints Go Marching In." "The way you and Daddy do it."

Louis turned to Red helplessly. "What do you put in this cat's milk?"

"Please, Dorothy," Red said.

"Just one chorus together," Dorothy piped, "then I'll go right home and go to bed. Even to sleep. I promise."

The jazz fans applauded both her remarks and her request for the raucous "Saints."

Armstrong picked up his horn and handed one to Red. "She sounds like an honest cat to me," he rumbled. "Let's lay it on her." To the audience, he said, "Ladies and gentlemen, a little exit music from the idol of a misled generation. The greatest horn in the country—Loring Red Nichols."

The "Saints" made the little place jump. After two choruses of the spirited jazz hymn, Red lifted Dorothy to his shoulders and started marching her around the club, singing. Just as he passed the front door, it opened and Bobbie entered, wearing her hat and coat. She had come from Vegas to the hotel, learned their whereabouts and gone straight to the club. Plainly she was in no mood to be talked to. Red marched to her, still singing, and out the open door. She followed.

By the time they got back to the hotel Dorothy was half asleep on Red's shoulders. He carried her to her bed, and returned to the living room to find Bobbie disapproving the disorder left by the poker-playing musicians. She sniffed the air and looked into ash trays.

Red knew what that meant and tried to distract her by gaily singing another chorus, softly.

"Home, sweet home," Bobbie said, sarcastically, when he stopped. "I won't stand for it, Red." Her nostrils sniffed the air again. "Who was using it?"

"None of my boys."

"Then keep the *other* boys out of here." She looked at the poker table and shook her head.

Red said, "Dorothy beat me out of forty peanuts. She cheats."

Bobbie wagged her head. "We've only got two choices, Loring. Either get Dorothy off the road or teach her to play a horn."

"What did I do that was so terrible?" Red asked. "She had a ball."

Bobbie went into the bedroom and Red followed. "I'll get her pajamas," she said. She started undressing the drowsy child. "Red," she whispered, "what about what you said to me the other day?"

"What did I say?"

"Oh, the same old malarkey about taking the band to New York and settling down."

Red sat down on the bed beside her and put an arm around her waist. "You know me like a book, don't you?"

"Right to the card that's stamped 'overdue.' Tony showed me the contract you signed extending the tour."

"I'll get her pajamas," Red volunteered, getting up to avoid the issue. "Then, after, I'll get yours." He got the pajamas and helped her put them on the child. "But, honey, it's a real fat deal. We're eating high on the hog. Mammy won't have to go around barefoot, no mo'."

"What about Dorothy?" Bobbie persisted. Neither saw the wide-awake child's ears perk up. "I know I may sound unreasonable, but until she's at least eight years old, I don't want my daughter singing in nightclubs."

"She'd knock 'em dead," Red said.

"What about school?"

"When she's old enough, sure. We'll get a tutor."

Bobbie shook her head. "I don't want her with the band any more. Next week they'll teach her how to smoke. Maybe marijuana."

Red let the marijuana crack slide. If the boys were hooked on it Bobbie was hipped on fighting it. While he never touched the stuff, he knew, and he knew that Bobbie knew, that it didn't make musicians stupid drunk like whisky. It gave them a lift. And while he didn't condone it, he didn't hate it as much as he did alcohol. He didn't drink on the job and he didn't think anyone could drink and play good music. And that went for the great Bix Beiderbecke, who had started drinking too much. Other musicians were killing Bix by having him play drunk. They would stand Beiderbecke up so loaded that he didn't know where he was, and force him to play—and laugh at him. Fortunately, Paul Whiteman had interceded and sent Beiderbecke away for a rest cure. But musicians weren't hurting Dorothy.

"Look, Bobbie, Dorothy loves music and she likes being with the fellas. Who says she's got to go to sleep when other kids go to sleep and get up when they get up?"

Bobbie put a hand on her hip. "I say. I want her to get up when other kids get up, at seven-thirty in the morning. I want her to have orange juice and oatmeal. Honestly, she thinks breakfast is black coffee and an aspirin."

Red turned Bobbie around to face him. "Listen, honey," he began softly. "We're on our way. All of us. Our records are selling like hot cakes. We're getting better playing dates and at better prices. Pretty soon we can pick our spots. And tonight I stood up in a club and Louis Armstrong said I was the best horn in the country. Imagine, Louis Armstrong—that's the Mahatma—the Supreme Court of Cats! I'll tell you something. I'm not! He is. Or maybe Bix, if he was sober. But maybe in a little while I could be—then we could pick the best hotel job in New York. Buy ourselves the best house on Long Island—fill it with oatmeal and orange juice, with a padded room for PTA meetings."

"When?"

"Soon."

"Why not now?"

"I just signed a contract. I couldn't get out of it if I wanted to."

Bobbie looked deep into his eyes. "Do you want to?"

Red stalled. "No," he said finally.

"Then maybe Dorothy and I should get that house and the oatmeal, and wait for you."

This horrified him. "And leave me alone on the road? What happened to the girl who wasn't going to let the baby change anything? The girl who wanted me to be happy doing what I'm doing?" He kissed her. "You know, for just a minute there you started to look like your mother."

Bobbie smiled at him. "I'm sorry. I guess I never really left Brooklyn—or Memphis."

If they hadn't been so engrossed in their problem, they might have noticed that Dorothy was listening.

Bobbie went on, "What's the answer, Loring?"

"Well, couldn't we put Dorothy in a boarding school, or something? Just for a little while?"

"Boarding school?"

"What's so terrible about that? It's not like when David Copperfield went. They've got some wonderful schools right here around San Francisco—big playgrounds, swings, swimming pools, tennis courts—and a couple of teachers, if you insist."

"Well, I don't know," Bobbie said. "Maybe when

she's ready, but I'll tell you one thing, it'd be on one condition."

"What?"

"That *you* tell her."

"Sure, I'd tell her. We're blood brothers."

Bobbie turned out the light and leaned over and kissed Dorothy. Red leaned over to kiss the child and Dorothy rolled away from him. Only then did he realize that the little poker player had been listening.

He couldn't do it to her. Not now. Bobbie had gone out of the room. Red spanked the child's bottom. "Okay, Blood Brother, you get a reprieve," he said. "No boarding school."

"Ala Kazam," Dorothy murmured and fell asleep.

In time they went back to New York and got that home out on Long Island. Bobbie made drapes and sewed and settled down to reasonable domesticity.

Red settled down to what the critics were going to call mediocrity.

CHAPTER 6

THE BOTTOM had dropped out of the stock market and it was a jittery New York to which Red returned in early 1930. Brokers were jumping out high windows, endangering the lives of former customers selling apples on the sidewalk. But demand for his music was still great, even from radio which he hated. The chains had grown. However, millions of radios were beginning to cut in on the sales of records, and the traveling band business was collapsing. For Red, the logical place to turn was to the stage. He had played in the pit of Earl Carroll's *Vanities,* and among his friends was George Gershwin who was about to launch *Strike Up the Band*. Red got the job leading the orchestra, and, they said, compromised with his ideals.

"It is a sad paradox," a jazz critic was to write, "that Red Nichols who built up such a great reputation with his Five Pennies, began to decline the moment his unique qualities were recognized and he was given jobs to play in the pit of musical comedies. These musical comedies, as musical comedies can sometimes be, were full of commercially successful tunes and Nichols, as pit band leader, was naturally expected to make recordings of these tunes, if only to give them authenticity. The recordings that Nichols made from the tunes in *Strike Up the Band* are excellent as commercial recordings. But as Red Nichols' recordings, they are rotten. One can trace in the arrangements and the performance, the weakening of Nichols' conscience."

Red was going to disagree with that. "Maybe one or two records are bad but, on the whole, the recordings of the tunes from the show are some of the best I've ever done." His motto always had been "Give people what they want," and he thought he was giving them what they wanted in recording the great Gershwin's music.

His next show, 1930-31, was Gershwin's *Girl Crazy*. For it he made up his mind to put together the best band possible, using some of his Pennies as a nucleus. Jimmy Dorsey wasn't available, so Red settled for Chicago Clarinetist Benny Goodman, a former Ted Lewis imitator who played for Ben Pollack, who had been influenced by the great Frank Teschemacher, and who had become a successful free-lance musician in New York. Red had used Goodman to record "Indiana" and, although their personalities clashed, he had a high regard for Benny's musicianship and thought he was in a class by himself on the clarinet. Included in the *Girl Crazy* band also were Glenn Miller, trumpeter Charlie Teagarden, and drummer Gene Krupa.

With those names, Red would make this the most talked about pit band on Broadway. It would represent a transition from the legitimate band to the jazz band for New York shows—a proper marriage of jazz and classical musicians inspired together by Gershwin's great music. It would be Red's masterpiece, something of which he would be proud.

He was proud. He was proud to go up to the businesslike Gershwin's apartment and discuss composition of "inserts" and "ride outs" to Gershwin's music and to go over the music with his Harmon-muted cornet. Because Red could sight read and transpose anything, Gershwin's skill would fascinate and inspire him; it would not awe him. He was proud to be taken by Gershwin to the Brooklyn Paramount and be asked what he thought of Ethel Merman who was singing there; because he thought she was great. He learned the next day that Gershwin had hired her for *Girl Crazy*. He was proud that Gershwin consulted him and took his suggestions. "I'd say, 'Why don't you have the band play the melody here and have Goodman play a jazz obbligato around it?'" Red reported, "and he'd do it." Red would take these suggestions to his own arranger, Glenn Miller, and Miller would arrange these inserts to go into Russell Bennett's score.

Red was proud, too, of Gershwin's confidence in him regarding his new drummer, Gene Krupa. Without that confidence, Krupa's career might have died aborning. Gene couldn't read music well and he made a lot of mistakes during rehearsals. "Get rid of him," Gershwin ordered.

Red knew that Krupa had a vast potential. He brooded over Gershwin's order. Gene and his drums were located in the pit behind those peerless readers, Glenn Miller and George Stell. Red had an idea. He went to Gershwin with it. "If we can be patient, he'll make it," he began. "I'm having Glenn wave behind his back to Krupa to signal change of tempos and such."

"All right," Gershwin said. "But if it doesn't work out after two weeks, let him go." This would give them time to break in a new drummer and not be stuck by the union's rules that after four weeks no man can be fired.

Day after day the frenetic young drummer, propped up by his peers, sat playing and watching Miller's back. A hand held one way said slower; another way, faster; a third way meant out. Meantime, Red was talking like a Dutch uncle to Gene. "Study, Gene; learn to read; learn the rudiments of those drums; get to know timpani." Gene did. His drum did a lot for the rhythm section. Before the show was six weeks old Krupa was playing the living hell out of those drums, blasting a path for his subsequent career.

That band at the Alvin Theater became the hottest thing on Broadway. It was the talk of the town.

But trouble was brewing. Red accused Goodman of making fun of the oboe player, of imitating his playing for laughs. Having had classical training himself from his father, Red had great respect for the oboist, a good legitimate musician. It was as though his father were being ridiculed. He told Goodman to cut out the horseplay. Goodman denied he was doing anything irregular. If the oboist had to play a passage that was corny to the ears of a jazz man, Red accused, Goodman was snickering and repeating it note for note, kernel for kernel. Finally Red went to the union asking that

Goodman be fired. The union sent a delegate to listen and watch for Goodman's alleged mischief. The delegate could not catch him.

Then Red was rushed to a hospital with acute appendicitis.

Pleurisy developed.

He was out of the band for several weeks.

Meantime, he and the band were given eight weeks' notice that the show was closing. One day, Glenn Miller telephoned him at home. "Red, Goodman has auditioned the band for Schwab and Mandel to play for *Free for All*," Miller said. "When we're through here we're going with Benny. Everybody except Krupa."

Red was thunderstruck. He couldn't believe it. *His* band, *his* masterpiece being taken over by someone else! His heart was in his mouth. Finally he said, "Fine. You might as well take Krupa, too."

"Oh, the theater has its own contract drummer—Johnny Williams—and will use him," Miller explained.

Nobody said "sorry," "tough luck, pal" or "what are your plans?" It was the law of the jungle. A new cat had risen to challenge the king. While the old cat was away the new cat had assumed leadership. And—worst of all—the little cats were going with him. It had happened in the jazz-band business before. A hot soloist would attract attention, decide to start his own band and take a few sidemen with him. Like amoebae, bands split up and multiplied.

"Never let them know how much it hurt you," Bobbie counseled.

Red couldn't help it. He was hurt and he was bitter. Had he been too hard on the boys? Not made enough allowances for errors? Expected too much? There didn't seem to be any animosity. Miller was friendly and casual in breaking the news to him. Red was a big man and perhaps the boys figured he could take care of himself.

While home recuperating, Red had signed a contract with Mickey Green to tour the New England "territories" and as far west as Pittsburgh. Now he had no band, was stuck with a contract. Maybe his sidemen simply hadn't wanted to travel, had preferred to stay in New York and work for Goodman.

"I was so bitter," Red said later, "that everything I tried failed."

Desperate for a good jazz band, he bumped into Milton "Mezz" Mesirow or Mezzrow, a "character" who had learned saxophone in jail, who played a little clarinet and supplied a lot of marijuana to musicians. Red had always considered Mezzrow a sort of "band boy" frequently deprecated by his Chicago contemporaries. Mezzrow was a white who called himself a "voluntary Negro" and who spoke the unintelligible jive of the "hep." Most important to Red, Mezz knew where Red could find a band quick. "Quit crackin' your jaw, daddy, and let me pull your coat," Mezz said. "I'll take the weight off." Among the players Mezzrow suggested were Pee Wee Russell, Pete Peterson, Dave Tough, Eddie Condon, Bud Freeman, Joe Sullivan, Tommy Coonan, a trumpeter, and Herb Taylor, trombone. The last two Red had used in *Strike Up the Band*. He knew that they and some of the others could read music and figured that they could carry the rest of Mezzrow's wild ear-pickers.

Red needed them. They needed money. Necessity made strange bedfellows—Red Nichols, the "paper" man, leading the so-called "hep," neither manifesting respect for the other.

After losing his pit band, Red was in no mood to cope with them. At the very start of the tour the men began grumbling about little things; of Red's attempts to discipline them both in their playing and in their dress and habits. They thought him a tyrant whose playing of Dixieland was corny. He, in turn, recoiled from some of the noises that came from their instruments. It wasn't a case of their discarding the melody to improvise, Red complained. To his exacting ear, it sounded as if they started off improvising and deliberately avoided the melody. Even if they all could have read to suit him, there was so much booze and marijuana around they couldn't have seen the notes for the haze. Cracking their knuckles as his father had his wouldn't have done any good. He wanted to crack their heads.

He was as embarrassed as he was angry. This was not the music for which he was noted. But he was powerless. Unless he could control the bad influence, Mezzrow, he could not control the band; and Mezzrow was uncontrollable. Worse, the college audiences were so drunk on prohibition booze they didn't know the difference. They applauded everything, encouraging the bad boys.

Finally, one afternoon during rehearsal—a stuffy formality to Mezzrow's "wild men"—Red decided to take no more from Mezzrow. Each musician had been provided with a pencil with which to make changes on his music but Mezzrow never used it and frequently kept blowing his clarinet when he was supposed to drop out. Red strode over to Mezzrow's music stand.

"When I say take something out, I mean out!" he snarled, picking up Mezzrow's pencil and crossing out the passage on his music.

Mezzrow raised his heavy lids and turned his glazed eyes on Red. "Daddy-o," he sighed elaborately, "why don't you light up and be somebody?"

The band roared with laughter.

Red was furious. He snatched Mezzrow's reefer and puffed it. It lifted him in a sort of daze. But it didn't make him *somebody* who could abide the strange sounds that came from that band. He threw the lighted butt back to his tormentor. "The whole damn band is fired," he stormed. "You're all on two weeks' notice."

The rest of the tour was canceled. And Red was in trouble. His best men had gone with Goodman. Other good men he had fired in a fit of anger because he hated their wild improvising. He was too proud to ask any of them to come back. Besides, he was afraid they would refuse.

The depression complicated his problem. Even if he had a good band, profitable bookings were hard to make. For about six weeks he loafed around New York, feeling sorry for himself.

The year was 1931. Billy Rose, Mort Dixon and Harry Warren had "I Found a Million Dollar Baby in a Five and Ten Cent Store" to head a torrent of music from Tin Pan Alley and its up-and-coming, now talking, challenger, Hollywood. Hit songs were a dime a dozen. They included "All of Me," "Barnacle Bill, the Sailor," "Between the Devil and the Deep Blue Sea," "Cuban Love Song," "Dancing in the Dark," "Goodnight, Sweetheart," "Lady of Spain," "Life Is Just a Bowl of Cherries," "Love Letters in the Sand," "Marta," "Minnie, the Moocher,"—the "Hi De Ho Song" of Cab Calloway, "Mood Indigo," "My Song," "The Night Was Made for Love," "Out of Nowhere," "The Peanut Vendor," "Prisoner of Love," "River, Stay Away from My Door," "Shadrack," "Wabash Moon," "When I Take My Sugar to Tea," "When Yuba Plays the Rhumba on the Tuba," "Where the Blue of the Night Meets the Gold of the Day," and "Yours Is My Heart Alone."

Big, sweet bands were coming up to play this new sweet music, adding to the hardships of the little, hot jazz groups.

And Red and Bix Beiderbecke—two bitter men—sat in Plunkett's, a jazz hangout also known as the Trombone for its steadiest patron, Tommy Dorsey—and commiserated with one another. Hard-drinking Bix had been sent away by "Pops" Whiteman for a drying out and had returned unable to hold his place in that band or any band. Big-hearted "Pops" had kept him on salary for almost a year. After the rest cure—which did not cure—Bix had gone home to Iowa for a time and returned to New York to try to hold down a job in Glen Gray's Casa Loma Band. His nerves were too shattered to cope with the band's difficult arrangements and he was fired. Now there was nothing to do but sit and drink at Plunkett's and feel sorry for himself. Sometimes he would have his horn with him and other musicians would get him drunk so he would play, then laugh when he missed notes.

To Red, who had been hurt himself by them, this was scandalous. He tried to get Bix to come and stay at his house but the proud little lone wolf declined. In the space of a year the great Bix Beiderbecke had fallen from the heights to ignominy. Musicians whom his playing had influenced and who knew they were inferior to him, now made fun of the man who had laid down so many soulful horn passages.

And because Red had a gnawing suspicion they were laughing at him too, he turned a sympathetic ear. "I know the situation, Red," Bix told him between hacking coughs. "It just seems like nobody—I know these guys wouldn't give me a quarter if I was starving. 'Pops' would take me back if—" He indicated the drink before him and did not finish.

Two days later he died of pneumonia.

Red decided not to kill himself drinking or waste time feeling sorry for himself. He would start all over again, from scratch. He had heard excellent little bands of college boys out in the "territories"—jazz groups which had come up with distinctive styles or with music strongly influenced by the jazz records of Oliver, Armstrong, Beiderbecke, Miff Mole and himself.

Leaving Bobbie and Dorothy at home, Red got into his band truck loaded with his books, some stock orchestrations, music stands and public address system, and started driving toward Lincoln, Nebraska, to organize a band with some college kids he had heard with Eddie Jungbluth earlier on a western junket.

At Harrisburg, Pa., he stopped, tired, bitter and sick at heart. He was alone. The road ahead would be long and hard. Even with experienced musicians, it would take months to hammer together a good band. With green college kids—

He telephoned Bobbie. "I can't do it," he cried over the phone. "I think I'll come home."

"Now, listen," she began sternly. "We discussed it and you made up your mind. You go out there and organize that band. You can't let those people down that you told you were coming. You can do it. Get them together, rehearse them and start out." She paused. "And remember we love you. We're in your corner."

As she had done before, Bobbie saved him. Without her he might have ended up badly, like some of the others. Unlike them, he'd always had a home to go to. His confidence buoyed, he got back into the truck and drove nearly all night. The quicker he got to Lincoln, the quicker Red Nichols and his many Pennies could start up the comeback trail.

The young musicians he had contacted were waiting for him, impressed that the great Red Nichols had chosen them, never realizing how desperately he needed them. Being young and ambitious, they were eager to please and would work cheaply enough to permit him to put together the kind of big band that then was becoming popular.

Also in Lincoln was a Swedish piano player and arranger named Manny Strand, whom the kids praised.

Red went to hear him play in a local theater and hired him, too. With Manny's skillful assistance, he chopped up and revised his stock orchestrations until he had about fifty good, simple numbers. For a month of rehearsals he hammered them into the boys. Some never had played rhumbas or the other Latin rhythms that were infiltrating the jazz and dance world, and which a good commercial band—or an "eating" band, as Red preferred to call it—had to play. But he got them in good enough shape to book them through Nebraska and Iowa. If he was taking corn to the corn country, he had the satisfaction of knowing that gut-bucket jazz was not popular here—did not have a wide following anywhere—and he was playing what the people wanted. The depression had turned jazz into back-room music and there wasn't much money in back rooms.

While Louis Armstrong toured Europe, Red and his kids toured the dancehalls of tank towns, then the larger towns and cities. He added a girl vocal trio, the Owens Sisters, and began playing nightclubs and hotels. Soon he was making enough to send for Bobbie and Dorothy and they began to travel with him again. By the summer of 1933, ten years after he made his Eastern debut at Atlantic City, he was back there again, at the Ritz Hotel, leading a big swing dance band. At Christmas, he was in the Claridge Hotel, in Memphis, Tennessee, and Bobbie went out to 782 Jefferson Street to look misty-eyed at her old home. For over a year more he traveled with increasing success, during which time one of his former Pennies, Jimmy Dorsey, was forming a band with Tommy.

Back in New York, he could give the back of his

hand and the sole of his foot to those who had counted him out. Up from the sticks, up by the bootstraps, up to a CBS radio contract, out to another home on Long Island. To go with his new, big, sweet band and his new dignity, he quit calling himself "Red." It was "Loring Nichols" when he began playing on the Kellogg College Prom show, starring Ruth Etting, which broadcast from colleges around the country. But it was the same Red when he was quarreling with Etting's husband-manager about how her accompaniments should be played, where Red should stand and how much Red should play.

Later he took over the summer show as a headliner, co-starring James Melton, and fought with Melton. Melton tried to conduct and made Red a nervous wreck. Finally one day Red stopped the band and said, "James, either you're going to be the conductor and the soloist or you're going to be the soloist and I the conductor." The ad agency, N. W. Ayers, backed Red up. When the series went off the air, Ayers gave Red the Frank Parker show for Atlantic Refining Co. While waiting for that show to start, Red booked into the State Theater in New York City and read an Abel review in *Variety* which said: "The augmented Red Nichols and his Five Pennies band (now numbering twelve, besides the trumpeting maestro) looms as something epochal in the evolution of dance bands as stage attractions. Nichols' is the first rhythm combo to click rousingly as a vaudfilm presentation. . . . This band has been three or four years ahead of itself. . . . Nichols is still a very young man whose jazz precocity three or four years ago, recorded on wax for the archives, at least gives him the unquestioned advantage of evidence that he pioneered the current swing vogue, and all the rest of it. So much so, that his then futuristic arrangements of 'Sheik of Araby,' 'Dinah,' 'Japanese Sandman,' and 'Avalon' on Brunswick Records, have been reissued again and again years after their first recording, and are as modern and fresh in 1935 as when first 'canned.' It is noteworthy that sitting-down audiences will accept and enthusiastically acclaim a rhythm combo such as Nichols', whereas it would have been a grave question a year or two ago."

When the Atlantic Family's rating began to fall, Ayers brought in a new comedian to bolster it. The comic was an immediate hit. When the series ended, he invited Red to join him in a show he was opening at the Paramount Theater.

Red turned him down. "I don't know why," he told Bobbie later. "I have no particular reason. I like him. We get along. Maybe I'm just getting cocky. After building the band back up and all, maybe I think I don't need anybody."

What had Variety *said? "Epochal ... click rousingly ... jazz precocity ... three or four years ahead of itself ... pioneered ... modern and fresh ... young man."* Who needs to tie up with a comedian?

The comedian went up and up, from one success to another. Red, who could have gone with him, went straight down.

He went on tour to capitalize on his radio following. People who had enjoyed sitting home listening to him on their radios still enjoyed sitting home listening to their radios. Money was so scarce that house managers, never too honest, short-changed him, miscounted the house or simply didn't pay him. Bobbie went along to help count the house; with her went Dorothy and a maid.

The box office almost ceased to exist. To save expenses, as well as finally get Dorothy off the road, Red broke the news to her that she would go to a boarding school. Red's father and mother had moved from Ogden to San Leandro, California, near the San Francisco Bay, and had bought a home. Dorothy would go into a school near them. Bobbie took her there and enrolled her, later rejoining Red on the road. Although the tour was losing money, the musician's union demanded that Red live up to his contracts. Bobbie sold her furs and her jewelry in order to pay expenses, and began driving the equipment truck.

Traveling lighter and faster without Dorothy and the maid, Red Nichols and his too many Pennies played unprofitable dates all over the country.

One rainy night in St. Louis, Red telephoned Dorothy's school from an airport phone booth and apologized for not being able to get to San Francisco for her birthday. "You understand, don't you?" he said.

"Dad, I wish you wouldn't call me up," Dorothy said. "It just makes me feel worse."

"Dorothy, Dorothy," Red yelled into the phone.

She did not answer. Red turned to Bobbie. "All the telephones seem to have gone out," he said, embarrassed and hurt.

Bobbie took the phone from him and listened. She heard it click. "No," she said softly. "I think it's just this one."

Jazz was being called "swing" now, getting its name from the effect that one musician could have on a band. In other words, did he "swing" from side to side? Did he wake up the band? Boogie-woogie was coming along, named for a style of piano playing—a rolling eight beats to the bar, left hand carrying the rhythm. In 1938, the night Benny Goodman was giving his famous jazz concert at Carnegie Hall, Red Nichols was playing a minor engagement in New Orleans. But the reviewer there was kind. "Red Nichols is our idea of a musician for whom the cornet was invented," he wrote. "From the smooth and soft legato passages he weaves into his version of 'L'Amour, Toujours l'Amour' to the snarling breaks he takes in 'Swamp Fire,' his maneuvers are sheer delight. When he decides to leave a melody to his orchestra and strike out on his own, his improvisations are shrewdly and spontaneously devised. But they never descend to that level of raucous and meaningless discordancy which seems so popular with many high-priced performers today. He preserves the thread of the music while adding to it decorations which seem quite logical when he projects them. He is, in short, a skilled and knowing artist who possesses an uncanny knack of developing intriguing rhythmic and tonal ideas."

Variety's reviewer in Milwaukee, not knowing how bitter Red was over this enforced, unprofitable tour, raked him over the coals February 21, 1940, for acting at Schroeder's, "as if it was beneath him to do a good job or even put forth a good effort to give the customers their money's worth. It was neither clever nor smart of Nichols to work a Sunday evening show dressed in a brown business suit, with his tie askew and a general carelessness in appearance. Neither was it good showmanship or good business to chew gum while leading the band; nor to clown around with the orchestra and ignore the people out front. At other times Nichols would walk off the bandstand and disappear for five or ten minutes, and then saunter back to take up the baton again."

By 1940, there were almost as many big swing bands as there were "jitterbugs" to dance to them. Although other big bands were still coming up, like Jimmy Dorsey's, Tommy Dorsey's, and Glenn Miller's, changes were in the wind. Intellectual interest in jazz was focusing interest on individual sidemen, pianists and singers in the big bands, with the result that new small combos starring these personalities were springing up. They called theirs "new" jazz, subsequently "modern," "progressive," et al. Rhythm sections were becoming more subtle. Musicians implied the beat instead of hammering it. Some of this music was sweet, some of it a cacophony of strange sounds. At the same time, on the West Coast, bands like Lu Watters' Yerba Buena organization, were trying to return jazz to its original New Orleans beat—a project which was to receive impetus a few years later when old trumpeter Bunk Johnson was resurrected from near poverty in New Orleans, provided with false teeth, and brought north.

Finally, after losing his shirt, Red had fulfilled the bad contracts. He and Tony were sending out feelers for new deals. Bobbie had had enough. She told Red so. "I gave up dancing to make a home for you. Now where is the home life? How can we have it on the road with you staying up all hours drinking with musicians and customers? You've got to give it up. We can go to California. You can make records in Hollywood and play in the little clubs around San Francisco, near Dorothy."

Red hesitated.

Bobbie began to cry. "I love you, but I'll leave you if you don't do it," Bobbie said.

Red saw that she meant it. He took her in his arms. He gave the band notice. Tony and several of the musicians decided to go to Hollywood and get work until Red was ready for them again.

Red rented a small house in San Leandro, a little farming community south of Oakland pungent with fields of garlic stretching up to rolling green hills. They took Dorothy out of private school and enrolled her in public school. She was underweight and having one cold after another. Now, with Red and Bobbie looking after her, she would get well. She would grow strong and tan in the sun and the country air. She would be repaid in full for all the time Red had spent away from her.

One day Dorothy came from swimming in a neighbor's pool complaining of a severe headache. Bobbie called a doctor. His diagnosis was appalling.

Polio! Meningitis! Encephalitis! All at once.

The doctor asked to be excused from treating her. "I've heard of only two cases like this and both died," he said.

He helped Bobbie get her to the Communicable Disease Ward of Alameda County Hospital.

Red was getting a haircut. A relative telephoned him. "Dorothy is dead," the voice on the telephone said.

With his hair half cut, Red tore the barber's apron from his neck and ran to his car. Dorothy dead! It was his fault! He had neglected her. If he had stayed with her and taken care of her she wouldn't have been in a weakened condition to get sick. The fact that two other cases of polio would develop from the same swimming pool would not ameliorate his self-condemnation.

Forty miles an hour. 50. 60. 70. 75. Red watched the speedometer creep up. A little twist of the wheel—a roll—and his problems could be over. A siren sounded. A motorcycle came alongside. A policeman shouted for him to pull over.

Red shook his head. "My daughter's dead. My daughter's dead," he cried out.

"Don't kill yourself," the policeman shouted. "Where you going?"

"Alameda County Hospital."

"Follow me."

With the siren opening the way for him, Red sped eighty miles an hour through traffic to the hospital.

He ran up the steps. "Where is she?" he stammered to the reception nurse.

"Are you Mr. Nichols?" she asked pleasantly.

He nodded violently.

She made a notation on a piece of paper in front of her, unconcerned. "Your daughter's doing as well as can be expected. We've got her in a respirator."

"She's not, not, not, not . . ." He couldn't say it.

"Mrs. Nichols is in with her," she said. "Would you

like to go in?" Through Red's brother-in-law, a doctor, she had gotten special permission for them to visit the contagious ward.

"Of course! Of course!" Red exclaimed.

The nurse led him down a corridor smelling of Lysol, creosote or some other antiseptic Red couldn't identify in his emotional state. Outside a glass door other people were waiting—people who had pulled strings to get in. A colored man and his wife, a Chinese woman and three white women. All wore worried looks. They did not speak.

"Wait here with these people," Red's nurse-guide said.

In a moment another nurse, looking tired and sad, came out from a room ahead. In crisp, efficient tones, she announced, "You are about to enter a contagious ward. Please stay three feet away from the patients at all times. Do not touch anything." She led them into a small room, almost a cage, and stopped.

Nervously pulling at his half-cut hair, Red had to restrain himself from running on ahead of her. She continued her instructions. "If you drop anything, do not pick it up. Do not touch the wall. Now follow me." She opened the door and started through. Red and the others followed.

The ward ahead was filled exclusively with children of all ages. Some were in beds, others in respirators whose electrically-driven bellows made whooshing noises as they forced diaphragms up and down, bringing life-giving air to their paralyzed occupants. Doctors and nurses moved soundlessly from one respirator to another administering to the children. At one end of the fat iron-pipe lungs mirrors were set at an angle above the heads of the children to make it easier for them to see a person standing over them.

At the far end of the room, Red saw Bobbie. She was standing at the end of a respirator, looking into its mirror at eye level. Red crossed hurriedly to her. Only Dorothy's face was visible, the rest of her being encased in the iron "boiler." She seemed to be asleep. Her breathing made her grimace painfully, forced on her in rhythmical cycles by the chugging electric motor beneath the lung. Bobbie looked weary, as though she had been standing a long time. She was silent, her face impassive.

Red crossed to her. "Hello," he said. He took her in his arms and kissed her and they clung to one another. "How is she?" he asked finally. Bobbie was unable to answer.

A doctor had crossed and stood beside them. Red looked up at the doctor. The doctor spoke. "I'd like to be more encouraging, Mr. Nichols. But she has gone into a coma. I'm afraid the chances are very slim."

Red had been holding Bobbie's hands. He dropped them and stepped toward the doctor savagely. "That's *your* opinion," he said.

"Not only mine," the doctor replied softly. "All the doctors on the staff." He couldn't bring himself to repeat what one had said, "I wouldn't give you a plugged nickel for her chances."

"Then get another staff," Red blurted. "Or another hospital." He spoke as though it were as simple as replacing a musician.

Bobbie put a finger to his lips.

Red drew his head away from her. "That's my daughter," he said to the doctor. "I'm not going to have you hang a number on her and give me the law of averages, and give up before you get started! If you don't know anything get somebody who does."

Suddenly he began to cry. He turned away, wiping his eyes, then wheeled back to the doctor. "Do something for her, will you, Doc?"

The nurse came over and motioned for them to leave. Bobbie took Red's arm and led him out. On his band tours Red had played many times for polio victims. He had visited the hospitals, in combination publicity-stunt-entertainment junkets arranged by the March of Dimes. He had even written a song for it which, however, had never been used. He had joked and talked to the little, recuperating patients without fully realizing what polio was.

Now that Dorothy had it, he knew. He wished he were dead. This was too big a price to pay for the music that he loved. He thought of Dorothy playing poker with the boys and staying up late hours to sing in clubs with him. He thought of how thin and sickly pale she looked when they first came to California. He would have given up every tune he had ever played, every record he had ever made, everything, to have this child well again.

Outside again, he and Bobbie kept vigil at the hospital far into the night. They were not alone, for polio was a big killer that year.

All night long a parade of grief-stricken parents came through the waiting room to take their turn going in. They didn't talk much to one another, but red-rimmed eyes exchanged mute glances of sympathy. White, black, yellow—the rich, the poor—the handsome, the homely—here, in common misery, they were the same. Once a smiling man came from the ward and spoke to the waiting parents. "My son's going to get well," he announced joyfully, telling them of his happiness and giving them confidence at the same time. Red glared at him, as if the man, by mentioning only his son, had given up the others as lost. "So's my Dorothy," he snapped, and didn't realize how brusque he sounded until Bobbie reached out and touched him and said softly, "Of course, dear."

They hadn't eaten all day. But Red would not leave. Finally Bobbie went out and came back with hamburgers for them. "There's an all-night stand right down at the corner," she said.

Red didn't answer. Bobbie opened the bag and started taking out the hamburgers. She nodded toward the ward. "Any word?"

Red shook his head.

She picked up the hamburgers. "Isn't it funny?" she said, trying to make conversation. "You live with a man for eight years and you forget whether he takes mustard or ketchup on his hamburgers."

"I'm not hungry," Red said.

Bobbie handed him a hamburger. "Now I remember, ketchup."

Mechanically Red took the sandwich. Bobbie started to eat hers. "Oh, go on, eat it," she said.

Red just stared at the hamburger in his hand. Tears came into Bobbie's eyes. "You know," she said, "I started out blaming you, too. The first few hours I hated you. Then I got to thinking. This could have happened no matter where Dorothy was. Even people who never let their children out of their back yards, this happens to them, too. Who can you blame? The whole world?"

"I can narrow it down better than that," Red said bitterly. "Do you know that every time we have traveled since we were married, every time I packed a bag, the first thing I always packed was my cornet. That'll give you a rough idea."

"Loring—" Bobbie couldn't finish.

Red bit into his sandwich. Across from him a woman stared at him as though to say, "How can you eat now?" It tasted like cardboard. He handed it to Bobbie. "I like mustard," he said.

"Sorry," she said, trading with him.

Red bit, chewed and swallowed mechanically. "I didn't mean to get sore like that at the doctor," he said, "but I've blown all my brains out through that horn since I was three years old."

"I know," Bobbie said. " 'Carnival in Venice,' Ogden, Utah. The Mormon Church festival."

"Unless some miracle occurs and that kid pulls through this, I'll never blow again."

"I didn't know you believed in miracles," she said.

"Right now there's very little else to believe in."

Bobbie handed him some French fries. "Remember the lyrics to 'Battle Hymn of the Republic'?"

"What brought that up?"

"It's been so long since either of us was at a church festival. It's like, well, a prayer. I thought it might do." She smiled. "It sold an awful lot of records."

Red shook his head numbly. "Can't think of it right now. Must have played it a hundred times, too."

Bobbie looked at the ceiling, her lips moving. "Mine eyes—have seen the glory—of the coming—of the Lord."

"Then there's a trumpet riff," Red put in. "You go back to the key of C. He is trampling—down the vintage—where the grapes of wrath—are stored." He shook his head. "Doesn't seem to fit here."

"It'll do," Bobbie said. "What's the rest?"

Red thought. "He has loosed—the awful lightning—"

Bobbie joined him. "Of His terrible—swift sword—His truth is marching on."

As they finished, the door of the ward opened. A nurse stepped out. "Mrs. Nichols," she called, "your daughter's asking for you."

The miracle! Bobbie was too startled to speak. Red sobbed for joy. He grabbed for Bobbie's hand, smashing her sandwich in his. "Put it down," he said. "You're always eating!" He took the sandwich from her and pulled her into the ward behind the nurse. A doctor stood beside Dorothy's respirator. In the iron lung's mirror Red and Bobbie saw Dorothy's face. Her eyes were open. They ran to her, calling her name. Bobbie tried to kiss the child but the nurse caught up with them and restrained her, again admonishing them not to touch anything.

Red grinned down at Dorothy, clasping one of his hands in the other to give her their old Ala Kazam, Kazam handshake. "Hi, Blood Brother," he said.

Dorothy turned her head wearily toward her mother. Red's smile faded. The doctor saw this. "Sorry," he said, "you'd better go now. We don't want to overdo it."

Dorothy's eyes pleaded with Bobbie. "Please, I'd like"—she labored to speak between the squeezing and suction action of the bellows on her rib cage—"my *mother*"—she emphasized mother—"to stay."

Red was hurt and embarrassed. Dorothy was old enough now to see him as he really was. She was blaming him for her condition. He had sacrificed her on the altar of jazz. He had thrown her through the blue smoke where the devil's music was played. To the frenetic beat of a viper's drum, he had offered up the child he loved. The grinning, sweat-drenched, tousle-haired gods had taken her. This was the penalty he must pay, both *her* rejection of him and *jazz's* rejection of him. His eyes glazed with tears. He turned and walked toward the door. It stuck. He yanked on it angrily. "Why don't they get some decent doors in this hospital?" he rasped. The door came open and he strode out.

Early the next morning while fog still lay over the Bay, Red left the car for Bobbie and hailed a cab. He ordered the driver to take him out onto the Golden Gate Bridge.

The cabbie looked at him curiously. "You just want to go *onto* the bridge? You don't want to go *across*?"

Red nodded and settled back in the seat.

"It's a long way," the driver said. "About ten dollars." He changed gears slowly and deliberately let a red traffic light stop him.

"What do you care?" Red grunted.

"If you gonna jump I want to be paid now."

It was an idea. But that was not his plan. He lifted his cornet case for the man to see. "I want to throw this over. Bury it deep."

The light changed and the cab crawled across the intersection. The driver looked in his rear view mirror at Red. "How do I know you're not a spy? And that's a bomb to blow up the bridge?"

Red passed the cornet and case up to him. "Get going. I haven't got all day."

The driver took the case and laid it on the seat beside him. "Yep," he said, "we get all kinds." He drove on in silence.

The fog was lifting when they got to the south end of the orange-colored suspension bridge. Below, whitecaps dotted the slate-gray water. A trim little Coast Guard cutter was heading out to sea, apparently to meet a Navy cruiser coming up the buoy-marked channel. The cab passed the south tower and soon was in the middle of the long high suspension. "Okay, buddy," the driver said slowing down, "here we are." He looked at his meter. "But before I stop I want $11.20—just in case you jump."

Red shrugged and handed him his billfold. "You can hold that as security," he said.

The driver stopped the cab. "Okay, make it snappy," he said, handing Red the cornet case. "I'm not supposed to stop here."

Red stepped out of the cab on the right side. The wind was strong and there was a slight swaying of the bridge under his feet. He stepped up on the curb and leaned over the bridge rail, holding the cornet far out from him.

"Careful you don't hit a boat. Or the seals." The cabbie's attempt at humor didn't amuse Red. He looked down at the water a moment, then turned the instrument loose.

He watched it fall, growing smaller and smaller. It took forever to reach the water. When it hit it made a soundless splash. Red continued looking down where it hit. Thirty years of his life lay buried at the bottom of San Francisco Bay. In an iron lung at Alameda County Hospital lay the rest of his life. He wouldn't need the horn to remind him of his long jazz career. Any time he needed to be reminded of the music his father had begged him not to play he could get this by looking at the crippled child the doctors said would never walk again.

The cab's horn sounded sharply. Red turned and went to it.

CHAPTER 7

IF HE WAS punishing himself by vowing never to play again unless Dorothy got well, at least it made him feel clean. Besides, there were more important things in the world than jazz. Germany, Italy and Japan had thrown the world into war. President Franklin Delano Roosevelt, serving his third term, signed the Lend-Lease Act to aid Britain and enunciated the four principles of human liberty known as the Four Freedoms—Freedom of Speech and Expression, Freedom of Worship, Freedom from Want and Freedom from Fear.

The United States wasn't in it yet, but it was only a matter of time. The whole San Francisco Bay area already looked like an armed camp with soldiers and sailors everywhere, and shipyards and steel mills working around the clock for the Lend-Lease program.

A little guy, only five feet seven inches tall, tipping the scales at one hundred twenty pounds, Red was classified 4-F by his draft board because of a hernia which forced him to wear a truss.

But manpower was desperately needed and Red desperately needed money. More than that, he needed an escape from himself, from the conscience that woke him up nights screaming for Dorothy to walk . . . please walk . . . just try . . . one step.

He applied for a job as a student welder at Pacific Bridge Shipyard in Alameda. He learned how to protect his eyes by never looking directly at the torch, and to wear a hard hat for safety against falling objects. He learned to tack-weld and to spot-weld. He learned to run a straight seam with the melting steel in a crack. He even learned to make it stick overhead, one of the most difficult jobs in the welder's art. He learned to protect his shoulders with the splash-leather guard worn like a football player's shoulder pad and he learned to operate a Union Melt machine, an ingenious device that crawled across the iron decks of huge ships, welding the plates together as easily as a sewing machine stitches cloth. He learned to watch the work lest moisture in the heated metal make bubbles which could weaken joints and cause ships to break up.

Meantime, Dorothy made excellent progress. She had been taken from the respirator and put in a rehabilitation ward with many other children. One day Red was on his way to see her, carrying a sack of toys, when he bumped into Tony. Tony gleefully announced that he had signed Red and the Pennies for a tour across country.

"Cancel it," Red said abruptly. Absorbed in his grief and his new job, he had completely forgotten Tony had been trying to find jobs for him.

"You can't do that," Tony exclaimed. "I've signed the contracts. They'll sue you for everything you should have saved the last ten years."

"Pay 'em off," Red said.

"With what?"

"That's your problem." Red fingered the toys he was carrying in the package. "Tell the boys we won't start up again."

Tony spread his hands helplessly. "You've been living like there was no income tax. You've got doctor bills like crazy—"

Red held up a toy mask to his face as though he had never heard. "Ever see anything like this?"

"Yeah—that waitress I was out with last night. Listen, Red—"

"Taxi?" Red saw a cab and started after it.

Tony followed him. "Come back. Listen."

Red reached the cab and turned. "You know what the doctors had the nerve to say to me? They had a big consultation and they said she'll never walk. Never, ever." He got into the cab. "You think I'm going to take that from them? Two of them are from Vienna. What do they know about Dorothy? What do they know about anything? I'll show them!"

Tony looked at him with understanding. "Sure, Red. Fire the hospital."

Red got in and slammed the cab door. He stuck his head out. "So long, pal."

"Wait a minute," Tony yelled. "I'm going with you." Red held out his hand. "It's been great, Tony."

Tony refused the handshake. "You finally got around to firing me?"

"Who else is left?"

Tony made a wry face. "Okay."

The cab driver touched his accelerator impatiently.

"Tony," Red said, "don't tell the boys anything about this, will you? You don't know where I am."

Tony nodded. "Sure, I never saw you before in my life." Now he took Red's hand. "So long—stranger. And don't worry about those doctors. Why, pretty soon they'll be working for you!"

Tony had remembered. As the cab pulled away Red waved back to his old friend and manager, a lump in his throat as big as a bass fiddle.

He went and picked up Bobbie and together they went to the hospital.

As he entered the rehabilitation ward carrying the toys, Red felt a sudden pang of conscience. This was not the ward where Dorothy was ill. It was a polio hospital in New Orleans. No, it was a crippled children's hospital in Cleveland. Or Milwaukee. He and his band were paying a visit to the kids, to play for them, to cheer them up—and more than incidentally—to have their pictures made for the newspapers. The song he had written for the March of Dimes campaign, but never used, ran dizzily through his mind.

Bobbie and a nurse were beside him, but he was hardly aware of them. How much different it was then. Then, he had joked and played with the crippled kids almost without feeling. Now he knew their every pain, their every sorrow.

"Hi, Red!"

"Hello, Mr. Nichols." The children's shouts shook him out of it. "Here I am, Red." "Mrs. Nichols, hello."

With his load of toys he was a welcome visitor. He was on friendly terms with all of them—except Dorothy. Halfway down the line of beds on the right she lay flat on her back, staring at the ceiling. She did not turn when Red and Bobbie came in. In the bed next to her was a boy, younger than she. As Red and Bobbie crossed toward her bed, the boy grasped the exercise rings above him and pulled himself up. "Hey, Red—look," he shouted.

"Easy, Billy," Red said. "You'll pull the roof down."

Bobbie clapped her hands together in mock amazement. "That's wonderful," she said, looking, however, toward Dorothy.

"I can do it only twice," Red said. His eyes were on Dorothy, too. "How you gettin' along with your roommate?"

Billy stared over at Dorothy, who ignored them with fine disdain. "Boy, you've got a strange one," he said. "Only exercise she's done since she's been here is when she tried to spit in my eye."

"Shut up." Dorothy's voice was a shot. She did not so much as cut her eyes toward them.

"There she goes again," Billy said.

Bobbie sat down on Dorothy's bed. "Hi, darling," she said. "Your father found a wonderful toy for you today."

Red made a big production of taking a toy monkey out of the sack in his arms and putting it on her bedtable. He wound it. "All you have to do is reach out and pull this switch. He'll play the cymbals for you."

"You know I can't reach." Dorothy's tone was flat—hopeless and accusing.

Bobbie feigned confidence. "The doctor says you could if you wanted to."

"Oh, sure," Dorothy grunted. "Easy as pie." She cut her eyes away.

Red and Bobbie exchanged glances. Dorothy was going to be difficult—again.

A girl on a neighboring bed called out to them. "Hey, how about our glee club?" the child asked.

"Not today," Red said, still watching Dorothy. He sat down on the foot of her bed. "I just don't feel like it."

Billy made a face. "Oh, brother, I guess it just runs in the family."

Red got up from the bed. "You fellas been practicing?" he asked.

Billy's reply was a high-pitched "mi mi mi mi."

"Don't call me," Red joked. "I'll call you."

From a bed far down the corridor a boy yelled, "Let's try 'Schnitzelbank' again."

Other children took it up. It became a chant. "Schnitzelbank, Schnitzelbank, Schnitzelbank."

"You'll never get it," Red said. "I beat you last time by two choruses and half a 'Schnitz.'"

He took a pitch pipe out of his pocket and blew on it. "Can anybody hit within a half a mile of that note?"

They all tried with varying results.

Now Red was Pagliacci. He sang with a broken heart, his eyes on Dorothy. "Schnitzelbank, bucking bronc, military man, dying swan." He went through antics appropriate to the lyrics.

"Old cowpoke?"

"Funny joke."

"Great big whirl?"

"Pretty girl."

105

"Odd machine?"

"Submarine," the kids chorused back.

"Rumpelstiltskin?"

"Very well, filtskin."

The children enjoyed it hugely. Red didn't think it was funny. Neither did Dorothy. She watched Red disapprovingly. "Why does he come down here and make a regular spectacle of himself?" she said to Bobbie.

Bobbie stopped singing. "I don't know," she said. "Maybe, for some strange reason, he likes to be around you."

"Oh, sure," Dorothy said, sarcastically. "Soon as I'm better I'll never see him again." She turned away and buried her face in her pillow.

Bobbie knew what she meant. But would he ever take to the road again? Rather, would he ever play again? She knew it took a strong lip to blow his kind of horn and Red was completely out of practice. He couldn't be happy working as a welder. He was being a martyr to his conscience.

Red continued making a spectacle of himself for Dorothy's benefit. Between choruses he stole glances at her to see if he was making headway. He was not. He nodded as a signal to Bobbie.

Bobbie took a photograph out of her purse. She held it up for Dorothy to look at.

"What's that?" Dorothy asked.

"It's to be your present—from that fella that's making a regular spectacle of himself."

"It's a house!" Dorothy exclaimed.

"We're going to live in one like it as soon as you get out of here," Bobbie said.

"All of us?" Dorothy asked cagily.

"All of us," Bobbie said. "All the time. Down in Los Angeles. Where the doctor says the climate's better for you."

Dorothy listened to the song a moment, then looked back at the photograph. "Our own whole house that's ours?"

"Ours and the First National Bank's."

"Our own towels?"

Bobbie smiled at her little experienced traveler. "It's a thought," she said.

Dorothy asked her to hold up the photograph again and she did.

Across the room Red saw that their plan was working. It was a photograph sent to him by a realtor friend in Los Angeles. He didn't have money for a house like that. For any house. But if it would help Dorothy get well, the lie was justified.

He went into another chorus of "Schnitzelbank" and stumbled through the words when he saw Dorothy's hands reach up for the rings.

Slowly she lifted herself up until she could see him.

For a moment their eyes met, then she let herself down.

He had won.

Dorothy would get well.

She had to.

Polio was an expensive disease. Charity, mainly through the Infantile Paralysis Foundation sponsored by President Roosevelt, took care of those patients who couldn't pay. Those who could pay, paid heavily. Red had paid until he was broke. The depression, bad investments, poor bookings, and a high style of living had left him in bad financial shape. Besides, he never had needed to save money. His security was in his horn. Pucker your lips, push the first valve down, push with your diaphragm. Push and blow. For a quarter of a century it had worked. Now it had failed. Without the horn, even the long hours of overtime which his lead man permitted him to work could not produce enough to pay their living expenses and take care of Dorothy.

Besides, his father lay slowly dying of cancer.

Desperate, Red screwed up his courage and went to the local bank to see if he could borrow money against his future prospects. "I don't have anything to offer as security," he told the man behind the low mahogany fence. "But I'm working hard and making pretty good money. I could pay back ten dollars a week, plus all I make from overtime."

The banker's mouth fell open. He scratched his head. "I don't like to tell folks how to run their affairs," he said, "but why don't you sell one of the lots?"

"Lots?"

"Yes. The ones your father bought."

"I don't get it," Red said.

"The lots he bought in your name." Thereupon the banker related a story that left Red crying. His father had bought a half dozen lots with the money Red had sent home to him every week, all in Red's name.

"If the going ever gets rough, son, you can always come back home."

The going was rough, and he was home. The investments had been the elder Nichols' full forgiveness of

Red for playing jazz. It also was his way of apologizing for having opposed the boy, of acknowledging that music with a beat—after all, not far removed from the marching music he played—had come to stay.

Red sold the lots and raised enough money to pay off all his debts and to put some aside for a down payment on a house.

Came the day to bring Dorothy home from the hospital. Red and Bobbie went for her in a taxi, carrying a folding wheel chair.

It was a happy moment and it was a sad moment. First they brought her toys out—most of them bed toys that could be played with without the use of legs. Then they put her in the wheel chair.

They pushed through the doors and started down the ramp from the hospital. Dorothy suddenly frowned. Red and Bobbie noticed it and knew how she felt. "That Billy in the next bed," Dorothy said. "I bet he's watching out the window."

Red and Bobbie drew a sigh of relief. "He seemed like a very nice boy," Bobbie said.

"You didn't sleep next to him for a couple of months," Dorothy said. "He knows everything. So I bet him a million dollars I'd walk out of this place."

"Oh, Dorothy," was all Bobbie could say. Red couldn't speak.

"I had to," Dorothy said. "He said I wouldn't ever walk again, ever. He said he heard the doctor say it." She looked up at Bobbie. "Did the doctor say it?"

Bobbie couldn't answer. Red bit his lip. Courage belonged to youth. He had had it once. If Dorothy had it now, he would have to get it. He threw his shoulders back. "Come on, baby," he said, taking Dorothy's arm. "Let's win that million bucks."

"Daddy, Daddy," Dorothy shouted. "You know I can't!"

Bobbie grabbed at Red. "Loring, you're out of your mind."

"We can lift her up, can't we? At least she won't have to leave sitting down." He looked at Dorothy. "Crazy Billy, what does he know?"

Bobbie saw his point. She leaned down and took Dorothy's other arm. Together they lifted her out of the wheel chair. They walked down the ramp with Dorothy's legs dangling helplessly. But she was not in a wheel chair. As they reached the taxi, they paused to open the door. Dorothy turned and looked back at the hospital. Triumphantly she waved. "Oh, I wish I could spit in his eye again," she said.

Red looked back and saw that a child's face was at the window. "You just did," he said, helping her into the taxi.

From that day on, Dorothy never quit trying to walk.

Prayer, exercise and Sister Kenny treatments filled her daily schedule. Bobbie, a believer in Christian Science, took her to her church's Sunday School and Dorothy began to develop a dogged faith and determination.

But one day Red detected Dorothy's spirits sagging as he prepared to apply the Sister Kenny hot packs to her legs. He had placed Dorothy on the kitchen table and laid newspapers on the floor in case he spilled water, and was lifting a boiling blanket out of a pot on the stove to run it through a wringer. He saw Dorothy shudder.

Make her laugh. "This is the best thing your mother ever cooked," he said. He picked up the woolen cloths by the corners and came toward her.

"Please don't put those hot things on me," Dorothy said. She moved a leg, protectively. It was a short move. Not more than an inch. But she had moved.

Red looked to see if Bobbie had noticed. She had. Her eyes were closed and she murmured a prayer. She said, "Dorothy, we have to. You've got to understand. We have to."

"You know they burn," Dorothy whimpered.

Bobbie kissed her while Red put the hot cloths on her legs. Still talking for Dorothy's benefit, he said to Bobbie, "I bet you think she's going to cry. Well, you're wrong. Nothing can make her cry. Can it?"

Dorothy gritted her teeth. "No—nothing."

After the hot packs had been administered, Bobbie and Red began massaging and moving Dorothy's legs at the knees. She cried out in pain.

Red went on making jokes too childish for such a big girl. "You think she's crying? No, that's a fake. When I was Dorothy's age, we had some kids on our block who were really criers. I remember fat Tommy, when he cried you could hear him for miles." He screwed up his face in a massive cry like the imaginary fat Tommy. "Then there was skinny Mildred. She could cry and sing at the same time. She was a singing crier." He put a hand to his breast like a prima donna and sang and cried at the same time.

"And there was a kid we called Meyer, the crier. How *he* got to Ogden, I'll never know. But every time he got the hiccups he used to cry." Red curled his lip into a cry and hiccupped at the same time. He stole a glance at Dorothy and saw her sobs had subsided somewhat; that she was listening.

"Did I ever tell you about Silent Sam?" he went on. "He used to cry without making any noise. Just made faces. Like this." He cried hugely and silently. "But the champ of the whole block was Joe Whiffenbeck. He cried like he was laughing and he laughed like he was crying. It sounded like this." He cried and laughed at the same time. Dorothy started to laugh, but then cried. She couldn't help it.

Red clucked. "Joe Whiffenbeck. Where have you been?"

"Walk—to move along on foot; to advance by steps; to go at a moderate pace; specifically, of two-legged creatures, to proceed without running, or lifting one foot entirely before the other foot touches the ground; sometimes, specifically, to move or go on foot for exercise or amusement."

The dictionary defined it well, but did not say how to do it. Red devised ingenious exercises to strengthen Dorothy's legs. He built a play area atop a hill back of their house, knowing she would have to crawl up it and he embedded chicken wire in the grass for her to grip while climbing. She crawled up it on her stomach, pulling herself with her hands, and using her legs as much as possible. He bought her a bulldog puppy, knowing that she would reach for it and have to use her legs to try to keep up with it. She crawled after the dog. She crawled up the hill. She would not let her parents help her and became angry if they tried.

"If you want me to walk, let me do it," she would say as she pulled herself along on all fours to the bathroom. She refused their help in getting into the tub, or in making her toilette. Her courage and determination, her little jutting chin amazed and saddened them.

"She'll walk," Bobbie said.

"Of course she will," Red would say, wondering if Bobbie really believed it.

But even if she remained a cripple, the exercise rigs that Red had installed made her a *happy* cripple. One was a trapeze with rings. Dorothy would hang on to it for hours, raising her leg as much as she could from the waist. It strengthened her arms, enabling her to perform feats of movement without her feet. Over a backyard fishpond Red built a steel bridge equipped with two hand rails. Gripping the rails Dorothy could drag her feet across the bridge. Time after time, day after day, month after month, she crossed this bridge. Red made a boat that would float the bulldog, now fully grown, and converted the bridge into a drawbridge which would open whenever she pressed a switch for the dog and boat to pass under, towed by a rope on a winch she worked with her feet.

One of the most ingenious exercisers was a Rube Goldberg contraption resembling a miner's sluice box that Red set up adjacent to the fishpond. Dorothy would sit at one end of the device, straddling a post in which were set stirrups in successive graduated notches. The object was to lift her foot as high as she could into the stirrup and press down. Bobbie sat beside her, encouraging her, while Red sat grinning fifteen feet away at the other end. Whenever her foot pushed the lever, it released a weight which in turn would release a ball; the ball would drop through a hole, roll down and trip another lever; a weight would drop, pulling the handle of a seltzer bottle and squirt Red in the face. Each time it squirted him he went through a different act, always keeping Dorothy in suspense as to what to expect. "Man the lifeboats; man overboard," he would yell as the water soaked his face and red hair. Again, eyes open to the stream, he would shout, "What a storm! I can't see a thing before me." Like most girls in their early teens, who haven't yet acquired a boy friend, Dorothy had a crush on her father.

He was father, sweetheart and idol rolled into one. Vaguely she remembered that Red also was interested in music, a creative artist a notch above the other welders who rode off to work with him in the mornings, wearing their funny hard hats, and who came home grimy and tired in the evenings. One day he gave her the scare of her life when another man drove him home and they had to help him into the house with his eyes closed.

"Daddy!" Dorothy screamed and fell down trying to get to him.

Red heard her and, although in great pain, opened his eyes to go to her and pick her up.

He closed them again. "It's only a flash, baby," he said.

One of the men explained this. "He's got little blisters in his eyes from looking at the arc."

"It's nothing," Red said. "Didn't start hurting until we were halfway home."

Bobbie heard as she came into the house from the back yard. She examined his eyes and saw that the blisters were small and not ulcerated.

She thanked the men for helping Red in and led him to the kitchen. She sat him in a chair and began grating a raw potato to make a poultice with which to draw out the pain.

The next thing both she and Red knew, Dorothy was standing before him, leaning on his chair, offering him a cold bottle of beer. How she had gotten it from the ice box, opened it and got it to him so quickly, they could only guess.

It was a happy guess.

CHAPTER 8

Now AMERICA was in the war. Music became less and less important to Red. There on the West Coast, in the shipyards, a new music was being played. Giant overhead cranes—long-legged metal spiders, straddling steel tracks—creaked and groaned under burdens dangling from windlass cables and dropped steel plate upon steel plate, to accent with massive cymbals the raucous rhythm of Rosie the Riveter's pneumatic hammers, while sputtering welding torches supplied muted arpeggios. Around the clock it played, set after set without rest, a continuous victory tune. By night the music was accompanied by the intermittent flare-ups of torches whose blinding blue light momentarily erased shadows thrown by the huge banks of overhead lights and washed swiftly over instruments of death being built for the Navy. The eerie blue raced across the smudged faces of old men and young men, of patriots and draft delayers and gold-brickers, of old women and young women and women who used the job to make contacts in more profitable pursuits.

But all worked hard. Navy vessels came down the

ways so frequently that launching ceremonies were dispensed with as a waste of time.

One afternoon, as Red Nichols straddled his Union Melt machine on the deck of a floating drydock in construction, his eyes behind dark glasses watched the continuous thread of molten metal unwind behind him, but his mind's eye was at home. There, Dorothy was having a birthday party. In the past he had missed many of her birthdays because he was on the road with the band. He would miss her sixteenth because, as people remarked to explain the unexplainable, there's a war on, and he was reluctant to take time off. He looked at his watch. If he hurried home as soon as he was off shift he could make the tail end of the party. Right about now Bobbie would be bringing in the cake with sixteen lighted candles on it. Dorothy would be sitting, her lower legs in metal braces, two aluminum canes beside her chair. Now Bobbie and Dorothy's friends would be standing, singing, "Stand up, stand up. Stand up and tell us your name," the birthday song they had sung to her for years. Slowly and with great difficulty, Dorothy would get up. . . .

The dining room was gaily decorated. Red, yellow and blue balloons hung from the ceiling. "Stand up, stand up. Stand up and tell us your name," the children sang. Dorothy painfully rose to her feet, holding to a card table for support, in front of a huge pink and white birthday cake with sixteen flickering candles. Bobbie stood to one side watching, too moved to sing.

Dorothy leaned forward and blew. Her wish was simple: To walk. Smoke rose from the candles as they went out. Now, bravely she let go of the table and stood alone, without assistance. As she spoke, pride and determination colored her words. "My name is Dorothy Nichols and I'm sixteen years old and I'm having a very happy birthday." The children applauded. Dorothy looked toward a handsome boy to her left and said, "And Richard Wilson, you had six helpings of ice cream so you're only getting half a piece of cake." She was joking, but it told Bobbie that boys now were important to her. Bobbie helped her cut the cake, saying, "Too bad you kids were too hungry to wait for Dorothy's father to get home."

"We can wait," a pimply faced teen-ager said, stuffing himself. "Bake another cake!"

Bobbie smiled wryly. It pained her that she had to lure the kids to the party with refreshments. Dorothy was not one of the gang. She couldn't jitterbug. She couldn't crowd around the corner juke box with them, drinking Coke and wolfing hamburgers. Although she could get around better she still was a cripple.

The boy Richard interrupted Bobbie's musing. "Hey, why don't we put on some records, and then we can all dance—" His voice trailed off and there was an embarrassed silence. He looked at Dorothy. Bobbie shrank back in fear of how Dorothy would react. But Dorothy herself saved the situation. "Sure," she said, seemingly unconcerned. "You kids go ahead and dance." She moved toward the phonograph with all the effort she could muster, ignoring the pain it gave her as she dragged one metal-encased leg after the other. "I'll change the records. Daddy's very fussy about them."

A girl who wore too much lipstick and rouge twisted after Dorothy. "Oh, one of those!" she exclaimed. "He probably blows his top if you play anything but 'Jeanie with the Light Brown Hair.'" The other kids laughed.

Bobbie raised her voice above the laughter. "You'd be surprised," she said. "You know, Mr. Nichols started the original Five Pennies."

"What's Five Pennies?" somebody asked.

Bobbie stopped in the midst of serving cake to a youth. "Am I getting that old?" she exclaimed, the question directed to herself.

Richard crossed to the phonograph beside Dorothy and searched through the records. "Is he hip enough to have some Benny Goodman?"

Bobbie followed him over. "All of them," she said. "Benny used to record with his band." Dorothy gave Bobbie the exasperating look that teen-agers reserve for unconforming mothers. "Oh, Mother," she sighed elaborately. "Don't put it on too thick! Benny Goodman!"

"Don't you remember?" Bobbie said. "He used to bring you candy."

"The *same* Benny Goodman?" Dorothy asked, incredulous. "How did he get so famous?" The other kids laughed.

Their laughter angered Bobbie and she had to fight for control. "You know who else worked for your father at one time or another? Jimmy Dorsey, Charlie

Teagarden, Gene Krupa, Glenn Miller, Tommy Dorsey..."

"... and Ludwig von Beethoven," Richard interrupted sarcastically. Now the kids roared. Bobbie could not hide her feelings. "Their names are all on the labels! Look at them!"

Dorothy looked about her, growing increasingly nervous. "Mother, how about some more punch, or cookies, or anything?"

Bobbie shook her head sadly. "You really *don't* remember, do you?"

Dorothy was apprehensive, not sure that Bobbie wasn't spreading it on. "Oh, I remember Dad used to have a band, and it was pretty good. But if it was *that* good, why in the world did he quit?"

Bobbie swallowed. Her eyes suddenly began burning. She let her gaze fall to Dorothy's braces. She closed her eyes, hearing again Red's vow in the hospital. "I guess you wouldn't believe that either," she said softly. She went to the door, away from the children.

Near the phonograph Richard wagged a finger in a jitterbug step. "Come on, Gates, let's jive. Give me some skin."

Dorothy put on a record. "I hear you callin'," she said, starting the machine.

A fast rhythmical tune filled the room. Richard gave it a try, found it satisfactory for his style of dancing.

A wave of nostalgia swept over Bobbie, choking her, as she listened. "Boneyard Shuffle—1926." She listened for the cornet and smiled proudly as it soared out of and above the band. "Sweet and pure," the critics had said. Even then Red was eliminating the harsh sounds from jazz. This was Dixieland as sweet as honeysuckle. A hot clarinet followed Red, mellow and intricate. Bobbie gave the kids a triumphant look. "For your information, that's Jimmy Dorsey on clarinet," she said.

The kids darted glances at one another, as though trying to decide whether to believe her. Bobbie put her hand on her hips. "The tune is 'Boneyard Shuffle' written by Hoagy Carmichael."

"The same Carmichael who wrote 'Stardust'?" somebody shouted above the music.

"Mr. Nichols recorded it to help Hoagy. Hoagy was just starting out and wrote to him asking advice." She listened attentively. "That's Dorothy's father on the cornet. Miff Mole is playing trombone. Artie Schutt on piano. The hot guitar you hear is Eddie Lang's. Vic Berton is stirring up that storm on the drums." She pointed to the stack of records Dorothy had uncovered. "Play 'em all," she said. "You'll find Artie Shaw in there too, if that means more to you." She turned and went out.

Now all the children were dancing. Richard turned to Dorothy. "If your father was such a hot shot bandleader, how come he's in my old man's car pool at the shipyard?"

Dorothy smiled thinly. "Oh, I don't know," she said. "You know my mother. She's way past thirty." She shrugged. "I guess she's getting senile."

Richard looked sympathetic. "Don't worry. They'll find a drug or something."

Down through the years, down through the records, they played on.

Although ships were skidding down the ways with such regularity that champagne christenings had been eliminated, the shipyard had all the appearance of a formal launching. Red, white and blue bunting hung from a wooden platform erected on a wharf beside a damaged Navy supply vessel which somebody told Red had been shot up in an attack on Guadalcanal.

Red reminded his informant to "zip his lip." "Besides," he added, "I happen to know the decorations are for my daughter's birthday party." He still was running the Union Melt, having already put in eight hours at overhead tack welding in the hold. Squatting on the crawling machine was restful by comparison.

Suddenly, above the clanging confusion of the busy yard, came the blare of a trumpet. Red cocked an ear. From the first four notes he identified the tune as an introduction to a familiar arrangement of "American Patrol." His machine reached the end of a seam. He stopped it and pushed up his dark safety glasses. They left white rings, inverted owl eyes, on his smudged face. He looked toward the speaker's platform in the distance and, from this vantage at the stern of the ship, could make out a banner reading, "Win the War With Ships." Beyond it, on a platform, members of an Army band sat holding their instruments poised to play. The opening trumpet soared to a crescendo. Now the leader raised his trombone skyward. All the brass joined in. Yet the trombone stood out, something familiar about its power and tonality.

"Like music, Loring?" His helper, a drawling young Okie, pulled the trailing cables out of the way for a return run down a new seam. He moved slowly, craning his neck toward the bandstand, keeping fast time to the music with a welding rod which he waved like a baton.

"Take it or leave it," Red said. *Especially leave it.* He listened a moment. "Drum's dragging."

"Sounds good t' me," the other man said. "Glenn Miller, he's tops in mah book."

Of course! Now he recognized the familiar sigh of that trombone. After Miff Mole and Jack Teagarden, Glenn was best in Red's book. "Miller's better at arranging, though," he said.

"Arrangin' what?"

"Skip it." If this kid didn't know that music was arranged, no use talking to him about Miff or Jack or Bix or Louis, or how Miller played second trombone so long for the Five Pennies. He probably never heard of the Pennies.

"American Patrol" ended with a crash. Workers going off and coming on shift stopped under the bandstand, cheering and applauding. Over a public address system, an announcer spoke. "Thank you, Captain Miller, for bringing your boys down to give us this show. And if some of our gang doesn't stop to listen, you know why. There's a war on, Captain! Ha, ha."

Captain? Now Red remembered hearing on the radio that Glenn had volunteered to entertain troops. That's what these grimy guys in the shipyard were, troops.

The announcer continued: "Before you hear from Glenn himself, I want to tell you a story by way of introducing some of the jazz he'll play for you. Seems that some Air Force brass complained about the jazz he plays, saying 'We played nothing but marches in the last war and we won it, didn't we?' Well, sir, Glenn came right back at him. 'Tell me, sir,' Glenn said, 'are you flying the same planes in this one as you did in that one?'"

Red grinned. Good old Glenn. Still sticking up for jazz. When had he first heard him? Summer of 1921? That was when Red, an Ogden dance band celebrity, had gone up to Salt Lake City with Ken Browning to hear Boyd Senner playing at the Louvre Cabaret, before cabarets became nightclubs. Glenn was going to college and was playing summer dances with Senner. Red took his silver cornet up with him and sat in a few times with the band. Years later Glenn had been a mainstay in Red's Broadway pit orchestra. While Red was going down, Glenn was going up. Why, they said, Glenn had made almost a million dollars already! With that many dollars he wouldn't remember the Pennies. Red frowned at his bad pun.

Over the public address speakers came Glenn's voice, interrupting Red's reverie. "We're happy to be here with you boys—and girls—who are building the ships," he said. "Your ships will ax the Axis. And speaking of jazz, we'd like to do a real oldie—one of the jazz classics from the good old days—as I used to play it with the famous 'Five Pennies.'" *He did remember.* Red had turned on his machine, but stopped to listen. "That jazz classic, ladies and gentlemen, is Red Nichols' great arrangement of 'Indiana.'"

Before the number could begin, a whistle blew, signaling the end of Red's overtime shift. He got up, stretched, put his gloves and safety glasses in his hip pocket, picked up his tin lunch pail, and started walking toward the bandstand behind which he had to pass to get to the exit. No time to wash up.

"Back home again in Indiana." The music came to his ears on a wave of nostalgia. Indiana. He was a green, cocky kid setting out to conquer the world with the Syncopating Five when they played in the state of Indiana. There he'd met a young law student named Hoagy Carmichael, a bad boy at school who loved music and threw chairs at phonographs when the music was bad and fell asleep playing the piano, who later had asked Red's advice about a career.

"Back home again in Indiana and it seems that I can see . . ." Bix Beiderbecke! See him and the Wolverines playing for Hoagy's fraternity house parties. Hoagy had insisted Red come hear the new kid from Iowa, this Beiderbecke whose hot cornet seemed to have a soul; this Leon Bismarck Beiderbecke whose exquisite tone and drive were matched by a melodic imagination suggesting the impressionists whose works he imitated; the frail, pasty-faced kid with dreamy eyes with whom Red would drink too much years later in New York; Bix, the legend who, Red felt, was killed by the musicians who stood him up to play drunk when he should have been in bed.

Red hurried across the shipyard behind the bandstand, unable to see the performers for the crowds of workmen pressing around, and unwilling to stop. If he hurried he could make the end of Dorothy's party. He went through the security gate, opening his lunch pail for the guard to look into and came upon a big bus parked outside. Red stopped to take the leather jacket off his arm and slip it on. Directly in his line of vision, the bus' sides bore a permanent engraved metal sign reading, GLENN MILLER AND HIS ORCHESTRA. Red saw that the bus was specially fitted as a rolling hotel room—a far cry from the speeding gypsy caravans in which he had made his one-night stands. During the last hard years of the depression, the Pennies had had to travel in several broken-down cars, Bobbie driving long overnight jumps to enable him to catch a little sleep. He began feeling sorry for himself, but thoughts of Dorothy dragging her feet and gasping for breath made him thankful he had this $80-and-overtime welding job.

As he stood before the silver trailer a breeze brought the music up to him . . . *"seems that I can see the gleaming candlelight still shining bright through the sycamores for me . . ."* There was his stocky little father handing him the key to his house, telling him, "If the going gets rough, son, you can always come back home." The bus became a canvas-covered spring wagon on which was crudely painted, *The Nichols Family Five—Instrumental Solos with Artistic Dancing*. The wagon jogged over desert roads with him, his sister and two half-sisters asleep inside, warmed by hot bricks under their blankets, his father huddled in the driver's seat scolding two plodding mules. Vividly his mind's eye saw again the yellowed press clippings from the Provo, Utah, Post: "August 8, 1912. THE NICHOLS FAMILY AT THE OPERA HOUSE. Master Loring, the seven-year-old son of Professor Nichols is sure a wonder and his work on the cornet is the talk of the town. Last evening, Loring gave a cornet solo, choosing for his number, 'Calvary.' A difficult piece for the best musicians, and his rendition of this was so very good that his audience was more than delighted. They were astonished at the ability of this young artist. Not only does Master Loring play, but he sings, and his songs are sung with much feeling and expression."

One of the trumpets in Miller's band hit a note slightly off and involuntarily Red put the back of his right hand to his lips. He imagined himself hitting a clinker and was feeling again the crack of his father's baton on his knuckles. Now he felt the razor strop on his bottom. His lips moved. "Papa, I got to play it," he heard himself say. "I can't help it. Besides, Lillian Thatcher pays me $1.50 when I play for her boys' band. That's a dollar more than you give me."

"Back home again in Indiana . . ." Now he was at Culver Military Academy, improving his playing under its Captain O'Callaghan, smoking forbidden cigarettes in his room while doodling with a mute to LaRocca's and Shield's Dixieland, shining upper classmen's shoes, getting his butt blistered by them because he was a freshman, because he was little, because he was young and cocky, didn't like military discipline and because he was a Mormon. The Mormons were unpopular in the midwest. From that section they had been driven in bloodshed only seventy-odd years before because of their beliefs and practices, including polygamy. In 1857, settled in Utah, they had retaliated against midwestern immigrants to California in the bloody Mountain Meadows massacre, in which Mormons and Indians killed one hundred twenty men, women and children. Although the Church made a good case for itself in disclaiming responsibility for

the deed, the fact that Mormons had participated in it brought federal troops and inflamed feeling against all Mormons.

"... *the new mown hay in all its fragrance in the fields I used to roam* ..." Red imagined he could see himself now in the trailer returning home to Ogden, expelled for smoking, a disgrace to his father, hero to young men about town. "Dance tomorrow, Washington's Birthday at the Berthana," the 1922 newspaper clipping said. "Jack Bowerings' Orchestra, featuring Loring Nichols on the Cornet. He'll just make you dance. No raise in admission." The toast of the town. Play pool by day, play cornet by night. Flunk your high school classes. Who needs a diploma? Why, Papa, I'm making more money now than you are!

Then ...

But, Papa, this is the chance of a lifetime. I'll run away! Harold Greenameyer will give me forty dollars a week and travel expenses to Piqua, Ohio. "*Well, son, if you've made up your mind. Godspeed. I don't want you going on as you have been, in poolhalls. I've equipped you as well as I could. Here's the key to my house. Take it with you. If the going ever ...*"

Miller's band changed tempo. Red reached into his pocket as though expecting to find the key. It was gone —and he had carried it so long! Funny how you lose the important mementos of your life and save the junk.

No, Papa, you don't need to go to the railroad station with me. Vic Thomas, the guitar player, you know, he'll go with me. We got a lot to talk about.

Dear Papa: I'm leaving Greenameyer to go with Ray Stilson to Lake James, Ind. He has a summer engagement there. I get $35 a week plus room and board. . . .

Dear Papa: I met a hot group here called the Syncopating Five and am joining up with them. We're going over to Chicago and will make some records for promotional purposes. Will cost us $25 apiece but will be worth it. . . .

Dear Papa: Now we are the Syncopating Seven. Johnny Hamp of the Kentucky Serenaders has booked the band into the Ambassador Hotel in Atlantic City, N. J. That's big-time, Papa. We had to change the name of the band to the Royal Palm Orchestra to get the job. We've got dignity and clean shirts and black suits and ties. . . .

Look, Papa, I'm back. You taught me straight. I wish my life could have gone as straight. Yes, Papa, Dorothy is better. She'll get well. So will you. You'll see.

No, son. You know better than that. Don't cry. You must be joyful when I die.

I can't, Papa. Sickness and death tear me to pieces. Why even when Dorothy had chicken pox in Cleveland it nearly killed me. And this other thing. And now you. No, I can't!

You must be joyful because my work is done. Why should there be tears on the end of your nose? There isn't anything that's going to bring me back. It's a normal procedure. It's a part of life. Life will go on and on. You'll die, too. Your mother is going to die. Your wife and child are going to die. Your grandchildren will die. This is the inevitable. Death is essential to life and life is essential to death.

Make no monument for me, son. Carve no stone. If you must mark the grave, put the shoes that I worked in at the head. Let the run-down heels and the holes in the soles say that I worked hard and did my best. Be grateful that my work and my mission is finished. Be joyful and play happy music.

"... *When I dream about the moonlight on the Wabash, then I long for my Indiana home....*"

Play happy music. Yes, Papa. Jazz *is* happy music. That's why I had to play it. You know that now. Jazz gave me a freedom of heart, an individual expression along the melodic line. I could change tempos and change the idea of a hymn—yes, Papa, the hymn—and make it a joyous thing. A joyous thing to dance to ... like the church teaches ... like we played in the Eighth Ward of the church back in Ogden.

At the trailer, another welder came up beside Red and stood looking at it. Red was not aware of his presence. His thoughts and Miller's music had become a single kaleidoscope flashing colored patterns out of the past.... New York ... the delicatessen where he and his Five Pennies improvised the "Indiana" melody from his own arrangement ... the nightclub where Louis Armstrong said ... "the greatest horn in the country—Loring 'Red' Nichols!"

The music raced into another familiar key change,

the saxes dominating. Red turned away from the trailer and started across the parking lot toward his car.

"Hey, where are you going?" the other welder called out. "Ain't you gonna stay for the music?"

"Naw," Red said over his shoulder. "I've heard it."

Heard it? He'd *lived* it.

CHAPTER 9

ARRIVING HOME, Red stopped his car in the driveway and got out. He started for the front door. At first he thought he still was hearing Miller's band playing "Indiana." But it sounded tinny and far away. He stopped behind the car, listening. Inside the house Dorothy's birthday party was in full swing, kids dancing and laughing. It was "Indiana" all right—*his* "Indiana." He craned his neck to see through a window. Well, what do you know! The kids were jitterbugging to it! He straightened up, swelling with pride. One-step, two-step, ragtime, jazz, swing, bop, boogie-woogie, jitterbug, swing—by any name it was the same. It was sweet, happy music that came from here, inside. Look at 'em bounce, shake, circle one another, push away, clasp hands and pull together again. Joy in their faces. *Joyful music*. The record was scratchy and thin. They didn't have the best of the new-fangled microphones in those days. The music was not as rich and full-bodied as Glenn's big band. But it was just as sweet and hot—and these young folks liked it! They were dancing to it.

He was about to bolt for the front door when the realization hit him like a cold shower. Dorothy wouldn't be dancing. She'd be sitting, laughing and watching, seeming to have the time of her life, but dying inside. He couldn't go in. He'd wait outside until they quit dancing.

". . . *Back home again in Indiana.*" Let's see. That's me and, uh, Leo McConville on trumpets. Trumpet mellower than the cornet, but cornet makes a better solo horn. Leo good all right. Record not so old, at that—Spring, 1929. It was a pleasant recording date. Made three masters, A, B, and C. All so good, hard to choose one for pressing. Sure! That's Miller there on second trombone; Jack Teagarden first. But Glenn will never catch Jack! Even if Jack did teach himself. Next to Miff, Jack is the most creative trombonist ever lived. Sang and made that trombone sing. Gave us a new trombone style. Believe I was the first to use him as a vocalist. Great individualist.

Diddle-de-dum-bum. Okay, Benny take a chorus. Blow that licorice stick. Benny Goodman. You don't have to acknowledge that it was in my Broadway show band and through my records that you started going places. As for *that other thing,* that's forgotten. But the music world knows that you and a lot of other big ones got your start with me.

Listen to the record. There's the proof. I gave you long solo parts. Not just four or eight bars, but a whole chorus of thirty-two. Listeners had a chance to judge how you thought on your instrument. I'm not being egotistical. It doesn't matter now—I got a little girl in there who can't dance. I brought you guys together,

Jack and Charlie Teagarden, you Benny, Jimmy and Tommy Dorsey, Glenn Miller and Joe Sullivan and I made you play in easy harmony as pleasant as your solos, and I loved you all and thought you were great. Through my recordings the Chicago and New York schools of jazz came together for the first time. And the critics said that was a big contribution. Critics! Ha! Know what my lead man said about my welding? Said I ran the longest and straightest weld on the day shift. Eighty bucks a week and overtime. And no promoters robbing you.

" . . . *Through the sycamores for me.*" Okay, step up Babe. Babe Russin. Tenor sax. Short, dark, mustache. Not an all-time great but well-educated musically— mainly self-taught. A California Rambler. One of the first tenor sax stars. Play anything, that boy. Read anything. Commercial.

Nice picking there, Karl. Karl Kress. Great guitar. Tunes it differently. Four strings. Great jazz heart. A ball-it-up, have-fun character.

Good rhythm, fellows. You too, Jack. Jack Russin, piano. And you, Gene, you're coming along. Gene Krupa. But, Gene, remember I said you gotta learn to read. Learn those drums. You miss sometimes. Hey, Glenn! Wave him out!

Good. Okay. Now let's get together for a finish . . . *"then I long for my Indiana home"* . . . diddle-dee-dip . . .

Red lit a cigarette and waited behind the car to see if the kids would quit dancing. He could hear them laughing and talking to one another but couldn't make out their words. Maybe they were laughing at the record! The thought froze him. They couldn't be. What was it *Downbeat Magazine* said? "The name 'Red Nichols' can always be relied upon to start a debate of some kind within rhythm club circles. Regardless of what you may think of Red Nichols' playing, the fact remains that he has been responsible for the production of a greater number of classic hot records than anybody in the business."

The music started again. Red relaxed. He felt warm inside. *"Ida, Sweet as Apple Ci-hi-hi-der. Room-roomp, room, roomp, room room."* Now there's *something*. Must have been the fall of '27. Sold a million records. And no wonder! Mighty rich and mellow for its day. Bobbie had been asking that we record something sweet for a change. Then Lennie Hayton, there on the piano, got this idea. He did the arrangement. First time the bass sax was used on the melodic line with harmony. Listen to it solo above, below and around the melody.

Ida, room room room room room. And the high priest of the bass sax himself, playing it. Adrian Rollini. Heard him first with the California Ramblers. Ambitious boy. Great jazz heart. Good drinker. Too bad he gave up the bass sax for the vibraphone and jazz for pop novelties. Sharp man with a dollar. Had his own club. Adrian's Tap Room in New York. Then into the real-estate business in Florida. Our pretty jazz captured later by Miller in "Peg o' My Heart" and "Tea for Two."

Lennie, you did all right, too. Formed your own band and became music director at a big movie studio. Married Lena Horne, became her pianist. Played and arranged for the best of 'em, Bix, Frankie Trumbauer, Whiteman, Bing Crosby.

The trombone behind Rollini caught Red's sharp ear. Miff Mole. Mole, in my view the greatest jazz trombone player the world has ever known! Heard him first with the Memphis Five and said he's for me. Followed his work with the Cotton Pickers and others. Finally met him when he was with Ray Miller and I was with the Cliquot Club Eskimos and hating every minute of it. Kind . . . humorous, lovable, thick-lensed glasses . . . Brooklyn accent. A former house painter who painted colors with his trombone in a new style . . . creative . . . perfect tone and taste. My idol. Had a sad life, too . . . too much to drink . . . sick . . . divorce . . .

That plaintive, low-down growl? That's the clarinet in the hands of Charles (Pee Wee) Russell. Heard him in St. Louis with Herbert Berger's band when I went out from New York on a short tour with Benny Krueger's band. One of the Chicago pioneers. Thought he was one of the greatest clarinet players I'd ever heard. Brought him into New York. Laid down some great jazz work, that boy. Started to booze it up so bad that I could use him only off and on. For some types of moaning blues he was the greatest. But drinking began to overshadow his ability. Damn it all, anyway. Why do jazz men think they have to drink to be jazz men? You can't play stoned. Nobody. I never could. Lose power and miss 'em. Bix, too. I had to sever professional relations with Pee Wee. Let's see. He was in a whole band I fired. He played on, frequently good, with Red McKenzie and Eddie Condon around 52nd Street.

Vic Berton. Extremely talented boy. Great drummer. Started as a kid like me. Well, of course! He named us! Why not call it Red Nichols and His Five Pennies? Great! That's it, Vic. Red Nichols and His Five Pennies. Vic introduced the "hot timpani," using a couple of machine kettledrums to play bass parts for novelty effects. Why, man, he could make a drum groan. And I guess he was the first drummer to move the cymbal off the bass drum to a stand of its own.

They were all playing together now. *Okay fellows, let's finish as a team* . . . 'deed I do. Vic! The cymbal close. Tuh-rimmmmmmmmmmp-ti-ti.

Inside the house the kids applauded. Red heard and wondered if the clapping was for the music or for some fancy step some kid had executed. Another tune began, thinner than the last. Red stepped over to the low front porch and sat down, his back to the music. The record was badly scratched but it was a racy number.

"That's No Bargain." Wrote it myself. Recorded late in 1926. Should have joined ASCAP then. Would have had something coming in from royalties on old tunes like that. Gosh, it's fast enough! Listen to those dancers jump, trying to keep up with it. Five of us. Me on cornet. Jimmy Dorsey, clarinet and alto sax; Artie Schutt, piano; Eddie Lang, guitar and Berton, drums.

True blue, Jimmy. One of the few who always credited me for boosting him along. Father was a coal miner who had a band and insisted that his sons,

Tommy and Jimmy, get out of the mines and amount to something. Jimmy was the younger, a quiet, serious lad. Heard him first when I was in Atlantic City. I was with the Royal Palm Orchestra and Jimmy and Tommy were with the sensational Scranton Sirens playing at the Apollo Theater. Man, that band knocked me on my fanny! Shy Jimmy, hot-headed Tommy. Funny how musicians' paths cross and recross. Hannah Williams—I sure flipped for her later—sang with the Sirens. Just a kid. But oh, you kid! Married Jack Dempsey.

That's *one* piano, man; not two. Artie Schutt just makes it sound that way. One of the greatest. What we call a two-handed player. Hard to find 'em nowadays. Scarce as snow worms. Nowadays it's all block chording and the player's left hand has to go the same way as his right. They'd never learn to rub their heads and pat their stomachs at the same time. If their right hand is going a million miles an hour their left is lying dormant down there thumping awkward bass notes. See 'em in the bars all the time, making a big thing of running up and down the keys with both hands together. That's all they can do. I'd just like to get some of the old ragtime piano parts out and have some of today's piano players look at 'em. They'd run, scared to death. Artie went out to California after working for me and became known as "The Baron," and something of a character. But he was great when he was working for me. His records speak for him.

What are you talking about, Ernest Loring Red Nichols? You threw your horn off the bridge. It's home for the barnacles now. You're a welder. A damn good one. You get eighty dollars and overtime every week. No more one night stands. No six-hundred-mile breakneck trips between engagements that killed so many sleepy musicians. No more blowing your brains—and your truss-supported guts—out. And your daughter is inside *watching* other kids have a ball. The daughter you neglected. The kid you and your damned horn turned into a cripple. Maybe you should have followed the horn off the bridge.

But how can you forget your music when somebody's playing it? Come to think of it—Bobbie was supposed to throw those records away. I told her to.

Hey, kids, dig that crazy guitar! That's real picking. The name's Lang. Eddie Lang. You never heard of him? Sure you did! Used to be Bing Crosby's accompanist. He died in 1933 when most of you were four or five years old. But let me tell you, you swingsters. Eddie was the first and the most on the jazz guitar. Interesting story about that pudgy little guy.

First heard him in 1923 at Atlantic City, too. Went over to the Knickerbocker Hotel one night for dinner and there were these two characters playing chamber music corn. You know, that candlelight stuff that's not supposed to interfere with your talk; about as personal as piped-in music. Eddie was playing guitar and his partner, Giuseppe Venuti, violin. I had studied violin and knew this guy was good. During intermission I introduced myself to them and invited them over sometime to hear us. They came one night and listened. Next time I went to dinner where they were playing, they asked me to meet them in the men's room during their first break.

I met them. Joe Venuti had tied his bow around his violin. "I can play your kind of music," he said, and darned if he didn't sail into "Runnin' Wild," then "Way Down Yonder in New Orleans," playing all four strings at once, making chords that way, while Lang chimed in with some of the greatest chord patterns I'd ever heard. I said then that if I ever got a band of my own, they would be mine. Shortly afterward, in the summer of '23, Johnny Johnson, who was playing at Asbury Park, asked me and Chuck Campbell to join his band. I did. Got seventy-five dollars a week and bought myself a raccoon coat (which I later had to sell for groceries). Anyhow, Johnson found himself with two contracts, one to play in Florida and the other sometime later at the Pelham Heath Inn in New York. He suggested I organize a band and take the Pelham Heath job. But meantime I had to live. Wil Paradise filled that gap. Sometime after I quit him, I got Venuti and went to Pelham Heath.

What a character that Venuti was. He loved practical jokes better than jazz. Once, for laughs, when he had finished his solo he sunk his teeth into his violin and chewed it up, spitting out the pieces on the bandstand. Some years later with Whiteman, he aimed a shotgun at the male singer whom he didn't like and had the guy trembling during his song for fear Joe would pull the trigger. And Beiderbecke told me the guy once built a bonfire of sheet music on a dance floor.

"That's No Bargain" ended and a couple of boys whistled appreciatively, loud enough for Red to hear.

Above the laughter came Bobbie's voice. "You haven't heard anything yet," she was saying, her tone proud. Then, as though she had been listening to Red's musings about Lang and Venuti, she put on "Bugle Call Rag," recorded in early 1927. Red remembered that it had been arranged to showcase Venuti's remarkable talents. Red on cornet and Dorsey on alto sax did the first few bars—just enough to justify the number's name—and from then on it was nearly all Venuti.

Sure, he'd thrown the cornet off the bridge. But how do you throw away memories?

"Bugle Call Rag" ended and was followed so quickly by "Nobody's Sweetheart" that Red knew someone was standing beside Dorothy's little phonograph ready to put the ghost record on. That's the way he and other musicians did in the old days. . . . Sitting around hotel rooms drinking and playing records . . . Everybody had a stack at least nine inches high and he'd take 'em around with him. . . . Bing Crosby, Charlie Teagarden, Jimmy Dorsey . . . They'd bring their stuff to my room and I'd take mine to theirs . . . Stand beside the phonograph and lift the needle to replay a passage we liked. Lots of times a man would be hired just because he *liked* a record you liked. You figured that if he had such deep appreciation of something good he probably could play it. New boys would come to town bringing records of unknown groups we'd never heard, records that they liked and records that they themselves had made. And you could play *all* the records in existence because there weren't millions of them in those days. A musician's one goal in life was to make a record, his next to play with a good band.

We listened to one another's records, studied styles and compared notes. No scientist ever studied another scientist's reports closer than we followed the hot licks on a horn. Yes, sir, when we weren't listening to records we were running out into the sticks to listen to obscure little bands in obscure little places about whom we had had reports. Out in the "territories," the trade called it. Up to Walled Lake, Michigan, or down to Indian Lake or out to Champaign, Ill., and hear guys that were playing in their college bands and they'd tear your heart out. Don't get that today. All you get is electronics. A guy plugs in a thing to a 110-volt socket and says I'll outplay anybody and he turns it up to a triple fortissimo and rattles your fillings. Guys like that with three guitars and an electric bass drown out a twenty-piece band and it's disgraceful. Too bad those little territorial bands didn't make records. The music they would have left would have been a heritage of jazz culture.

He'd reminisced so long that "Nobody's Sweetheart" had finished without his consciously thinking about it. But his retentive ear still heard it and played it over for him. It was on the sweet side, because of the low key arrangement and the addition of Whatshisname Fosdick's fine melophone. He had striven for these "pretty" sounds as a relief from the monotony of blowing straight jazz. After four hours on a bandstand playing the same stuff, your ears get tired.

"Rose of Washington Square" began to blast out to Red on the front porch and he heard the scraping of many feet on the floor, swinging to its galloping rhythm. His ear counted the instruments. Ten men—

McConville and himself on trumpet; Jack Teagarden and Glenn Miller, trombones; Pee Wee Russell, clarinet; Bud Freeman, tenor sax. . . .

Freeman. Developed into a fine tenor saxophonist with a highly personal style. Came up with the famous Austin High School crowd out of Chicago with Jimmy and Dick McPartland and the renowned Frank Teschemacher. Believe Eddie Condon said Freeman was the first tenor sax man he ever liked. Didn't read well. Used to play with Dave Tough out in Grant Park in Chicago when nobody would let 'em play indoors. One of Mezzrow's wild crowd which included Pee Wee Russell that I fired because I couldn't control them. Bud turned out the best of all of them. Recorded with his own group, won a couple of important jazz polls.

And—think of the devil—there are his cohorts, Eddie Condon, punishing the banjo, and Dave Tough, slamming the drums. Ah, Eddie. A legend in music but a musician? A good promoter for jazz but maybe not such a good jazz man. Sharp sense of humor that doesn't quit. A great talker, great fun. Taught himself to play the ukulele and banjo. Played with Red McKenzie and was one of the founders of the Chicago school of jazz. Came to New York fresh out of Chicago after he and McKenzie had made a hit record of "Nobody's Sweetheart." He and McKenzie were going to set the world on fire. Couldn't get a job except in 52nd Street joints. Condon, known as "Slick." Heavy drinker. McKenzie played a comb. Another of the group, Josh Billings, got very interesting drum sounds out of a suitcase. Condon was an Irish wit and iconoclast. Because he couldn't read note one, he poked fun at all who could. When you fire a band you fire everybody in it. He went out with Mezzrow.

So did Tough—and that's what hurts you years later. Davey undoubtedly was the greatest jazz drummer that ever lived. Small, frail, sick, mixed up, drinking heavily, moved in and out of the musical scene but always tops when he was jumping behind the drums big as himself. Well-educated. Well-read. You had to like Dave.

"Ice cream, everybody!" Bobbie's cry stopped the music and the dancing. "But no more cake. We've got to save a piece for Mr. Nichols." Red made it his cue to enter.

"Daddy!" Dorothy's shriek was filled with laughter and love. Red crossed the room to where she sat beside the phonograph.

He kissed her. "Happy birthday," he said. He nodded toward a dusty stack of records. "Where'd you find those?" He made his tone casual.

Bobbie moved quickly beside him. "In the attic," she said.

"I thought I told you to throw them out." He studied the children's faces, trying to decide whether they had been enjoying them or putting up with them.

A fuzzy-faced youth standing close to Dorothy—too close, Red thought—spoke up in an octave-hurdling voice that was changing from a squeak to a grunt. "Sure glad you didn't. Some of them are pretty funny."

Red wheeled on him, but caught himself. "Yeah," he said sourly. "They're hilarious."

The boy laughed, failing to catch Red's sarcasm. "Say, Mr. Nichols, was that really you on that old trumpet?" he asked.

"What trumpet?" Red pretended ignorance lest they learn he had been sitting outside listening.

"Oh, on 'Ida, Sweet as Apple Cider' and that 'Boneyard Shuffle' thing." He indicated the records.

"No," Red said.

"Why, Loring . . ." Bobbie interrupted.

"Not on those numbers," Red went on. "The instrument was not a trumpet. It was known as a cornet." While he always had preferred the cornet for fast tunes because of its smooth mechanics, he had used the trumpet on many mellower numbers.

"Cornet! Whoops!" The young idiot's mouth flew wide open and he slapped a hand to the top of his head. The other children joined his laughter.

"They still have a few in the Smithsonian—beside the pedal organs," Red growled. He felt his face flushing and he knew that Bobbie would see he was angry. He shrugged and tried to laugh. It sounded hollow. "They're saving a place for me there."

Dorothy got up and stepped, laboriously, between her father and the boy. "Sure, that was Dad playing," she said. She smiled proudly at Red. "I can remember."

Red felt his anger drain out of him. He grinned broadly at Bobbie. "Dig that cat," he said.

Dorothy faced the boy. "He *was* good," she said. "He played just like Harry James!"

Red moved around to face her. "Harry James plays something like *me* . . . only not enough." His tone was emphatic, defensive.

Dorothy backed away, almost stumbling. Red reached for her but she motioned him away. "Oh, sure," she said. "Harry James plays like *you*."

Red made the youth his target. "You heard me!" he snarled.

The boy put up his hands in surrender. "We believe you."

Red looked over the crowd of kids and jabbed his shortened valving forefinger at one after another as he spoke. "There was Bix . . . and there was Louis . . . and there was me . . . and that was it. And remember it!"

The children regarded him curiously. The fuzzy-faced youth backed away from him. "Yes, sir," he said nervously. "You and Bix and Louis. That's it. We'll remember."

Another boy, skinny and with a crew cut, bobbed his head like he was going for Hallowe'en apples. "Mr. Nichols," he croaked, "my father used to listen to you all the time. He told me all about you."

Red let that soak in on the other kids. "Well, that's *something*," he said.

The skinny kid's head bobbed again. "He said you were smart to get out of the business before the parade passed you by."

Pass me? Variety said I was always four or five years ahead. He glared at the youth and bobbed his head in imitation with him. "I've got a message for your father, but you're not old enough to deliver it!"

Dorothy became alarmed. "Dad, would you like to lie down and take a rest?"

Red ignored her. "If I had a horn here, I'd show you

kids something." He heard a boy ask, "Can he play the *new* kind of jazz?" and Red could have slapped him.

He felt something touch his elbow. He turned and saw it was a cornet in Bobbie's hand. She was looking up at him enigmatically. "Will this do?" she asked.

Red caught the spark in her eyes. He took the instrument and examined it. "It's my old one that Papa was keeping," he said. He peered into the bell self-consciously as though expecting something to jump out of it. "What's it doing here?" His tone was urgent. Had his father taken a turn for the worse?

Bobbie put a finger against the horn and idly traced a circle. "Before he left town, Tony went over to see your father. He sent it by Tony." She stuck a tongue in her cheek. "He thought some member of the family should start playing."

"Hummmph!" Red said. He looked at the kids, then at the horn in his hands as though it were a hot dish he wanted to set down. There was no place to put it. He put it to his lips. His cheeks puffed out. A high note rang from the bell but promptly flattened out.

There was an embarrassing silence. Red's fuzzy-faced tormentor turned from the group and headed for the door, past Dorothy. "I got homework," he said to the group. Under his breath he added to her, "Is he always like this?" The other children fell in behind him like startled sheep, and headed for the door, murmuring nervous good-bys.

Red jumped in front of them, feeling as ridiculous as he looked. "Nobody leave this room!" he rasped, angry at himself and them.

"Daddy!" Dorothy's voice whined and reprimanded. She clamped her hands to her head in abysmal shame.

Nothing could stop him now. He snarled at the youths. In a broad sense, they represented one of his troubles. They were the jitterbugging, swinging generation that didn't know that Dixieland was the pure jazz, the basic beat, the roots, the sustenance, the father, the mother, the heart, the soul of the music to which they danced. Without his jazz there would be no "swing," no "new" music, and the college kids wouldn't be inventing words like "progressive" and "modern." And if these tin-eared stumblers had a single emotion in their awkward bodies—pale shapes like cookies not quite done—they would shun the "modern" and "progressive" false queens who were worshiped only because they were new.

Don't they know that simplicity is the essence of both invention and good taste? If an automobile has seven hundred parts and I can eliminate two hundred, that's progress. If I *add* two hundred parts, as so-called progressive music adds to its unharmonious chassis, that's not progression; that's retrogression.

First off, music requires an *understandable* melodic line. Then you have *understanding* between the player and listener. I can go down the street whistling harmonic notes around a melody and only I understand them. They satisfy me because I have the unuttered melody in *mind*. Let someone else play those same notes without in some way announcing the melody to me beforehand and I don't get it. That's so-called modern and progressive music. I don't get *it* either. It's a bunch of complicated scales with no relationship to anything I can identify; no foundation that I can see.

Red took a step toward the youngsters and they backed away from him. These were the kids who listened to musicians playing the same thing over and over—boodle boodle bubble bubble bubble bubble—and accepted it as music, not knowing it was little more than an exercise in composition. It was not jazz. It was out in left field. It was the left-fielder playing baseball without the other eight men and a batter. Bach's fugues they even tried to work in as progressive. But that's old; it's *counterpoint* and makes sense. The world's complicated enough without complicating the culture of music, which is an international literature itself. I can take my horn and go anywhere in the world and I can play a song and people will know that it's a song. They'll know the meaning behind it. I can do that with *one* instrument. The more you use the more complicated it gets. Nobody in progressive or modern music has small, four-, five-, six- or seven-piece combinations that are going to sound like Stravinsky's "Firebird" or "Petrouchka." There's a place for progress but it must be *progressive* progress, not jazz played backwards. You can't monkey with the heart that is put into the playing of an instrument. That's the culture of music. When it's played with the right feeling and format and even though you're not conscious of what you're doing, it's a culture within yourself that does not transcend the scope of human feeling. I used to carry "Petrouchka" around with me all the time. One little passage I copied note for note in a thing I wrote. I listen to symphonies and enjoy them because they are confined to the laws of music. I believe in law.

When laws become inadequate, I believe in changing them. But I don't believe in changing them for no reason.

"Daddy?"

"Huh?"

"Loring, are you all right?"

"Sure, Bobbie." Red smiled at Dorothy. He looked from face to face in the group before him. He held up his cornet. For a lifetime, he had fought this battle with the mad improvisers of jazz, with the reefer-smokers and alcoholics who threw away the melody because they couldn't follow it, who couldn't create anything around it or add anything to it without destroying it. And he wasn't going to let these damp-behind-the-ears kids leave with the wrong impression of him.

"Look, kids," he began. "You come here, drink my Cokes, eat my peanut-butter sandwiches. The least you can do is listen."

Dorothy didn't appreciate his attempt to joke. "You don't have to *prove* anything," she scolded. "We believe you."

"Sure—whatever you say—we believe you," a boy chimed in.

A girl giggled. A boy coughed dryly.

Red lifted the cornet to his lips. A sharp, clear high note stopped the youngsters short. They quit laughing and looked at one another.

Red hit another. And another. The run of notes fell together into an arpeggio. A distinctive melody began to form. It was his old theme song, "Wail to the Wind."

The kids didn't know it but Bobbie recognized it

immediately. She hurried to the piano to accompany him, bursting with pride and happiness. Dorothy was getting better. Red was going to be himself again, too. A little rusty on the valve work but nothing that practice couldn't cure.

The children were open-mouthed and speechless. As Red reached for higher and higher notes their heads seemed to reach with him. He hit a piercing crescendo. Then, fffflllllubbbbbbbb. The note soured and collapsed. His futile breath making no sound through the horn added to its ludicrousness. A girl tittered.

Red pulled the cornet down. His lip was split wide open. Blood gushed from it.

"Loring!" Bobbie screamed. She jumped up and helped him dab at the lip with a handkerchief.

He looked at the blood on the handkerchief, then at his embarrassed audience. "Sorry," he murmured through stiff lips. "It's been so long—lip soft. . . ."

The children avoided his eyes.

Dorothy began to cry softly. "Oh please, Dad," she sobbed. "Don't make it worse by explaining."

Red closed his eyes. The cornet slid out of his hand and clanked onto the floor. He heard the children leaving. He did not open his eyes until the last one had gone through the door. Then he turned slowly and walked toward his room.

Bobbie looked after him. Her heart was filled with love and pity for him. She stooped and picked up the cornet. She fondled it tenderly, as though it were his heart.

CHAPTER 10

Bobbie stood the cornet on its bell atop the piano and went to the door with Dorothy and her guests. When the children were gone, Dorothy began to cry. Bobbie patted the child's cheek and reminded her that her father had been under a severe strain in changing his life from that of an applauded public figure to an anonymous shipyard welder.

"He didn't have to break up my party," Dorothy pouted.

"I'm glad he did it," Bobbie said. "You'll be glad, too, when you understand."

Bobbie listened for Red in the back of the house and heard him showering. He was not singing as was his custom.

Men, Bobbie reasoned, all have three faces. One they show to the world at large, another to their wives and families, another to their colleagues and close friends. She had seen all three of Red's.

The first face she had seen in New York in the early twenties—that of a dashing young man-about-town, loving the limelight in which he found himself, impressed by the prominent people who called him by his first name—Gershwin; Babe Ruth; Texas Guinan, the nightclub operator who made "Hello, sucker" a byword along Broadway; her brother, Tommy; the Williams Sisters; politicians in Tammany Hall; George Raft, who was doing a Charleston act with Texas; Earl Carroll, whose *Vanities* pit band he had led and, when he went up to Harlem, Armstrong, Fletcher Henderson, Willie the Lion Smith, Coleman Hawkins and little Fats Waller.

A handsome little guy with flaming red wavy hair, an easy smile and alternately serious and laughing eyes, he could get more girls than was good for him. He had always been surrounded by women—his stepmother and his three sisters; three girl friends at school and, when he hit New York, the chorus girls. With the latter he was like a kid in a toy store unable to decide which bright bauble to play with first. The fact that his eagerness was ill-concealed at first by his country boy manners and dress made him just that more attractive to them, especially to Bobbie whose Southern-lady background overshadowed her profession as a chorus girl.

While Red bathed, Bobbie fixed dinner and reminisced. Her mother had died at her birth down in Memphis, and she had been reared by her uncle and his wife who taught the child to call her mother. He was a contractor and builder who had built schoolhouses and courthouses in Virginia and Indiana. One of his daughters married and moved away to New York and his wife wanted to be near her. The family moved there when

Bobbie was fourteen and soon afterwards the father died. Bobbie had been given the regulation "advantages," including acrobatic dancing. When she was offered a job in a chorus back in 1918 she convinced her mother that a girl could do backbends, cartwheels, splits and one-two-three kicks on a stage without necessarily going to hell in a handbasket.

In 1919 she danced in *Floradora*. She once did a number with Cliff "Ukulele Ike" Edwards and, with Frank Faye, led the famous Equity strike of actors. She had been offered a chance to come to Hollywood in *Big Boy* with Al Jolson, but her mother wouldn't let her. And she was glad. Because it wasn't long before Loring Nichols appeared on the New York scene, fresh out of Ogden by way of Ohio, Illinois, Indiana, Atlantic City and Asbury Park, with a soulful horn and a roving eye.

After their first date to go up to hear Armstrong in Harlem, she learned that several other girls in the chorus were chasing after Red—heard them raving about him in the dressing rooms. One night when she was on the stage she heard Red, playing in the pit, whisper to Hannah Williams that he would meet her outside. Bobbie knew that Red had virtually taught Hannah and her sister Dorothy to sing by having them repeat notes which he blew on his cornet—knew that Hannah had something of a crush on him. Their meeting outside didn't set well with Bobbie; Red had just told her he wouldn't be able to see her that evening.

After the show Bobbie went outside too, and saw Red and Hannah waving for a cab. She waved too, and when a cab came she jumped in it and went home without a look back. All night Red telephoned her. Her mother said, "Any man who'll call a girl at these hours has no respect for her." Bobbie told him to make up his mind—"It's either me or them." He made up his mind. It had been Bobbie ever since.

After that he saw her every day until they were married. He'd do crazy, romantic things—like ride home with her to Brooklyn in a cab, then insist she ride back to New York with him.

"You wouldn't want me to go alone, would you?" he'd pout, and Bobbie would ride back with him. There, he'd say, "But now how'll you get home? I guess I'd better go back with you." And he would while the cabbie shook his head in wonderment and watched the meter with delight.

One day, after they were married, Red came home and announced that they were going to Europe. Jazz had made a big hit over there and he was in demand because of his records. In fact, anybody who could keep time and play loudly could pass as a jazz musician in Paris, so hungry were Europeans for this new music. Often they kept better record of the musicians than the musician kept of himself.

In order to get Red's passport, Bobbie sent home to Ogden for his birth certificate. It came back, plainly revealing that Red was two years younger than he had told her he was. She blew up.

Said he, "I was afraid you wouldn't marry me if you knew the truth."

With him talking like that, she couldn't hold the lie against him—even if he had put her in the "awkward" position of being two years older than her husband.

Bobbie had not met Red's parents. They learned of the marriage from a story in *Variety*. The show business paper said that Red had married a chorus girl—"a woman"—older than he. Bobbie had noticed he wasn't getting letters from home. "Don't you write to your parents? Don't they write you?" she asked.

She could see the picture the parents got. Not only had he been expelled for smoking and had flunked his studies to play pool, but now he had come to a no-good end. He had married a painted woman who was a labor agitator and who danced for that man Carroll who gave that wild champagne party at his theater. She attended the party with their boy and, horror of horrors, had been subpoenaed to testify at Carroll's trial. It never would occur to them that she could not testify to anything of importance because she had gone, like some of the other girls, on Carroll's command and had left before the girl in question swam in the tub of champagne.

Bobbie sat down and wrote his mother. She told her how happy she and Red were. She described how she was decorating their home and enclosed samples of material with which she herself was making curtains, bedspreads and vanity covers. She also told her of the new dresses she was making herself. Meantime, Red's sister, Dorothy, for whom their Dorothy later was named, was digging in, trying to learn the facts about this unholy union.

Moran and Mack, the Two Black Crows of stage, radio and recording fame, had worked in shows with Bobbie and knew her well. When they got to the Golden Gate Theater in San Francisco, Dorothy went in to see them. "Tell me about *this woman* Loring married," she demanded. Moran, the little one, looked at her and said, "Well, you should know her. There's only one thing I can say to you: I don't know how your brother got her."

Bobbie got this later from Dorothy herself. Dorothy said she reported this information to her mother. She quoted Mrs. Nichols as saying, "Well, I just got a letter. She sews and makes things. Regardless of what stories we hear, just from this, she sounds like a good girl."

That was the beginning of a long understanding between mother and daughter-in-law. His family decided that Bobbie was good for him. "I felt I had been given a trust," she said. And they got along so well that people began to say it wasn't normal; they should fight.

Red needed considerable "house-breaking." Living in hotels, he had dropped dirty clothes and towels wherever he happened to be. His musician friends, Bix Beiderbecke, Eddie Condon, Glenn Miller, Jimmy Dorsey and Bing Crosby would come to the house and play records and drink for hours, burning holes in her rugs and coffee tables and spilling drinks on her beautiful new piano. They were all bachelors except Miller, who sometimes brought his wife, Helen. They were young, irresponsible and a pain in the neck to a meticulous housewife. She took it out on Loring, made it so miserable for him that the rowdies quit coming. Whenever he played where musicians were smoking marijuana she made him air out his clothes before coming into the house. "A lot of your friends are drifting away, and it's my fault," she often told him. "Forget it," he'd say. "It's you I want and I want you happy. The others don't count."

This was his second face revealing itself. It was the face Bobbie liked best. Red depended on her for nearly everything. He asked her advice and usually followed it. The money was rolling in—and out—as if there were no tomorrow. One day he bought her a mink coat, a silver fox, a diamond watch and a string of sables all at once. They had a beautiful home in Long Island.

Even little Dorothy was aware of the fuss women made over Red. It seemed to the child that every time a certain girl singer spoke to Red she put an arm around him. Dorothy put a stop to it. "Can't you talk to my daddy without putting your arms around him?" she demanded.

Once when Red was playing a big Kansas City hotel dining room, Bobbie, asleep upstairs with Dorothy, got a telephone call from a woman around 2 a.m., shortly after the band had quit for the night.

"Is Red there?" the caller asked.

"No," Bobbie replied. "You might try the manager's room. He may be having a nightcap with him or some of the musicians or a guest."

A half hour later the woman called again. "I've telephoned everywhere and I can't find him," she said, now quite cross about it.

"Keep looking," Bobbie told her. "He's around somewhere. If he comes in I'll have him wait for your next call."

All night long, until 5 a.m., the woman kept calling. "I don't understand it," she complained bitterly. "He had an engagement with me. I don't like being stood up."

By then Bobbie was too wide awake to sleep. "Well, I'm waiting for him too," she said. "If you'd like to come up and sit and wait with me, I'd love to have you."

"Say!" the caller exploded. "Who are you, anyhow?"

"Mrs. Nichols," Bobbie said.

"His mother?"

"No, his wife." The noise of a slammed-down receiver hurt Bobbie's ear but did her morale a lot of good. If Red was avoiding women like that—even if he might be boozing it up somewhere else—she had little to worry about.

Red's dependence on her, coupled with his strange fear of and distaste for sickness of any kind, made Bobbie feel she had to stay well for his sake, and she believed Christian Science philosophy helped her to do this. His parents had told her that Red's phobia could be traced to the time when, as a small boy, he saw his father brought into the house on a stretcher, collapsed from overwork. The incident caused him to run away, not to be found until late at night. Then a short time later he had thrown a lighted match into a pan of gasoline, suffering burns so serious it was feared he might die or lose his legs.

All his life illness had upset him. Merely hearing that Jimmy Dorsey was having one operation after another for his hernias, believed caused by blowing too hard to play, could panic Red; he had a hernia, too, but never could bear surgery. When he had to be operated on for appendicitis, it upset him as much as learning he had lost his band.

He leaned on Bobbie for courage in building up another band and he leaned on her when he was planning a tour to capitalize on his radio popularity—the tour that failed and led him to the shipyards. At that time he told Bobbie, "I want you to stand at the head of the stairs where you can hear offers these men are going to make so we can talk about them later." Bobbie listened. She recommended taking the first man's offer. Red didn't take it and blamed his subsequent misfortune on his failure to heed her advice.

The chicken pox Dorothy had in Cleveland had upset Red to the point of making him ill. Her polio floored him. It was fear of facing the dismal truth about her prospects more than his own stubbornness that made him refuse to believe the doctors' opinions.

While he was breaking under the strain, bawling out doctors, Bobbie was keeping an even keel. When she was a little girl she had broken both arms between wrist and elbow at different times and both got well. Her mother had read of Christian Science beliefs and without joining the church had practiced a philosophy of doctor-*and*-faith healing. Bobbie believed in that too, and frequently had sent Dorothy to Christian Science Sunday School.

In Red's determination to make her well again he could never match the dogged resolve of the child herself. They had obtained her release to go home only after a nurse had called at the Nichols home to see that they had the proper facilities for treatment—a bed with boards under the mattress, woolens for heat packs, etc. Dorothy resented the bed boards. She would crawl out of bed on her hands and knees to sleep anywhere else. Before she could half walk, she insisted on riding her bicycle. Bobbie would try to stop her. "Mother," the child would say, "do you want me to be an invalid, or do you want me to get well?" Put to her that way, Bobbie let the child do as much as she physically could do. Bobbie was afraid the hospital would hear that Dorothy was doing more than she should and that she would be taken back to the institution for stricter supervision. To prevent this she found a registered nurse to testify that Dorothy was under her care, reassuring the hospital. She also was afraid the hospital would misunderstand hers and Dorothy's Christian Science philosophy. "So many people *do* misunderstand," she said. Neighbors, for instance, raised eyebrows at the occasional visits of the Christian Science practitioner, and Bobbie had to explain that he simply prayed with them, as a visiting priest or preacher might do. "We are strong," she would say, "but we need this outside prayer and comfort because we cannot bear our burden alone." Red, the Mormon, once misunderstood for his beliefs, went along with this, convinced of the value of prayer.

Dorothy would not let anyone drive her to school. She walked, perspiration dripping from her, up and down hill, gasping for breath because the paralysis still was in her chest and throat as well as her legs. It also affected her tongue muscle with the result that she frequently swallowed it. Once her tongue fell back while she was in an automobile going twenty-five miles an hour, and she jumped out and fell, gasping for breath.

Bobbie stopped the car and pulled her tongue back.

Another time this happened when Dorothy was downstairs preparing for bed. Her big English bulldog was upstairs with Bobbie. The dog hated the stairs which were slippery. It came to Bobbie begging to be carried down, as was its custom. Bobbie sent the dog away several times but it persisted. Finally Bobbie picked up the dog, all eighty pounds of it, and carried it down. The dog ran to Dorothy. Bobbie followed. There was Dorothy, leaning on the dresser, gasping for air. Quickly Bobbie reached into the child's mouth and grabbed her tongue. Dorothy, out of her senses, bit her mother's fingers. They bled profusely and carried the scars for several years.

Hearing of things like that, seeing Dorothy grimace in pain, shattered Red.

That, too, was his second face—the face of the man who needed comforting, the man unsure of himself.

His third face Bobbie had not seen often. But she had seen it enough to know it was there. This was the face of the music perfectionist who expected his sidemen to be as note-perfect as he. Musicians complained that he made little allowance for error and that he was hard on them in other ways. On the bandstand he would not let them smoke or drink and insisted that they be dressed alike, usually in dark suits, white shirts and black ties. On the subject of jazz he was dogmatic.

This third face he had worn when he addressed Dorothy's birthday guests.

It told Bobbie that music still was in his heart. She was glad.

CHAPTER 11

IT WAS SUNDAY—one of the rare Sundays that Red was not asked to work. The shipyard had found that men must rest a day every now and then, even in wartime. Weary workers were not efficient and there was the danger that a sleepy man would fall and kill himself.

Red awoke at 8 a.m., but stayed in bed until Bobbie and Dorothy went off to Sunday School. Not only was he bone tired but he still felt embarrassment from his conduct at Dorothy's birthday party the afternoon before. He came into the living room, took the morning paper away from Dorothy's big English bulldog which was chewing on it, and sat down to read. The old silver cornet which Bobbie had left on the piano caught his eye. He looked away from it at the paper but his eye kept straying back. Finally he got up, went over and picked it up. He started to put it to his lip when he remembered the split. He went to the bathroom and cut a small piece of adhesive tape and stuck it over the split. He came back into the living room and put the cornet to his lips.

Across the room the dog lay with one eye open,

watching him. Before a sound came from the horn he got up, grunted elaborately, and waddled out of the room.

"Critic," Red hissed after him.

The dog's action gave him time to think of what he was about to do. Hadn't he given up music forever? Didn't he vow never to play again unless Dorothy got well? Was she well? No.

He put the cornet back on the piano and sat down to read again. Again his eyes strayed to it. He got up, took it to a back room and threw it up into a closet and closed the door on it. He went back and continued reading in peace. He heard the sharp click of the dog's claws on the polished floor and looked up to see it come back in and lie down.

Bobbie and Dorothy returned from Sunday School, panting. "She's walking better," Bobbie said, her eyes going to the piano. She looked down at Red. "Where is it?"

Red hid his face in the paper. "Threw it off the bridge," he said. "It can play duets with the other one. Maybe the sharks will like it."

"Quit feeling sorry for yourself." It was Dorothy speaking, not Bobbie.

Red glanced up to deny the charge. Dorothy was almost out of the room, her back to him. He saw that she was walking with less limp. He forgot what he was going to say.

Bobbie's eyes went from Dorothy to him. "She walked three miles," she said.

"It's been warm," Red said. "Maybe the doctor's right about Los Angeles being better for her."

Los Angeles—four hundred miles to the south—had more sun, less fog and wind.

"Let's go," Bobbie said. "We could get a little house there and"—she paused—"and you could get into a shipyard or an airplane factory."

He got a week-end off and they went to Los Angeles on their wedding anniversary. Bobbie had made him promise to take them to see the sights. One of the sights turned out to be the Brown Derby restaurant in Hollywood.

Red was suspicious. He knew musicians hung out there, near the broadcasting and recording studios, and he didn't want to see any of them. From the sidewalk he looked up at the Derby hat which served as a roof. "Idiotville, U. S. A.," he mused. "And the Brown Derby is the capitol. Why do you want to go there?"

"Because you promised," Bobbie said, steering him toward the door. Somebody passed them coming out. "Oh, look, isn't that Clark Gable?" she exclaimed.

"It's the Brown Derby, isn't it?" Red grunted without looking to see. He looked into the glass in the door, straightening his tie and jacket before pushing it open. A queue of tourists stood at the maitre d's stand, waiting for tables.

Dorothy was wide-eyed. She stood between her parents, where her leg braces would be least noticeable, and drank in the sights. Handsome men and women sat at the booths. All around behind them the walls were completely covered with framed caricatures of famous Hollywood personalities. "Let's sit where we can see all the movie stars," Dorothy said.

Red craned his neck to look under a booth table. "You mean under the table?"

"Oh, Father!" Dorothy reprimanded.

Red shrugged. "If you knew how I hate these places." He caught the maitre d's eye finally. "Table for three, please."

"What name?" the tuxedoed man said mechanically.

"Nichols. Loring *Nobody* Nichols."

The man pursed his lips. "There's a half-hour wait," he said.

"Can I try another name?" Red quipped.

The headwaiter looked blank and walked away with a couple to a booth.

"Paisano!"

Only Tony Valani would shout like that. Red turned. "Hey, Red!" Tony was coming toward him.

Red shot a glance at Bobbie which said this was a put-up job.

Tony put out his hand to him. "Could it be? From out of the blue!" he exclaimed at the top of his voice.

"Hello, Tony," Red said quietly, ignoring Tony's hand.

Tony spread his hands in a gesture of defeat. "You don't see a guy for years, that's the best you can do, 'Hello, Tony'? Not even a handshake?"

Bobbie leaned forward and kissed him resoundingly. "Hello," she said, smiling warmly.

"Now *that's* what I call a handshake," Tony brightened.

He smiled at Dorothy and she said, "Hello, Mr. Valani."

Red leaned back, eyeing them suspiciously.

"Hi, Dorothy," Tony said, taking her arm. He waved a hand toward the line of booths. "Come on—sit at my table. I'm handling bands for the Morris Office now. They pick up all the checks. I spend all my time eating."

They pushed past the maitre d' who now smiled at Red. "You know," Tony went on, "this must be a miracle or something. Just today I was talking to some of the big boys about you. What the music business needs right now is another Red Nichols."

Red looked at Bobbie, her averted eyes confirming his suspicions. "If they can't find a hole in the head," he said. They reached the table and Red saw at a glance that it was set for four.

"You expecting the Andrews Sisters?" He fixed Dorothy with a look. "As for you, you don't even *like* movie stars."

Bobbie touched Red's elbow and tried without success to push him into the booth. "All right, Loring," she said. "It was a plot. I heard Tony was here and I called him."

Tony beamed. "And glad I am she did. Of course, I can't start you right off at Carnegie Hall, Red, but there's a little club in a hotel downtown—it's a beginning—"

"Not for me," Red said. He turned to Bobbie and Dorothy. "Let's go."

"Red—" Tony's voice was pleading now.

Red shook his head. "That was another fellow, Tony. Forget it."

"Red!" It was a new voice and it rang through the dining room. "Red, man, where've you been?"

Red turned back. Jimmy Dorsey was seated in a booth with a group of men who had the mark of musicians on them—pale, esthetic, sleepy-eyed. Their coats matched their trousers and told Red they were easterners, some of the hundreds who came to dodge the cold and to pick up a living in the booming record business.

To Bobbie Red said, "How could you do this to me?" To Jimmy he said quietly, "Hello, Jimmy."

Dorsey looked good, only older, grayer and heavier, his clothes richer. "And *Bobbie!*" Jimmy went on exclaiming. "And is that *Dorothy?* What are you doing with Tony? I thought you gave up the business for good?"

Red straightened his tie crisply. "Just passing through on the way to Hawaii," he said. "We fly over and take a ship back. Some folks take the ship over and fly back. Not us. After living it up over there, we need the rest of an ocean voyage."

"Yeah," Bobbie said dryly. "We've been on the beach for years."

"Retired, huh?" one of Dorsey's companions put in.

"Nothing to do but clip coupons," Red said.

"I never thought any member of the union ever made it," Jimmy said.

I'll bet a bale of last year's arrangements you never, Red thought. *You've made it and you know damn well you have! Glenn Miller made it too. You think I don't see the papers?*

Red looked at Bobbie. She shook her head ever so slightly. He put a fist to his mouth and coughed into it. "Well, Jimmy," Red went on. "I don't take all the credit. After all, Tony here was my business manager all those years." He put an arm around Tony, his fingers pinching Tony's upper arm as hard as he could squeeze. Tony laughed to keep from screaming in pain. "Yes, sir," Red continued. "You know how well Tony takes care of his clients." He looked at his watch. "Well —got to see my broker."

Dorsey gestured for them to sit down at his table. "How about lunch?"

A waiter came up with Dorsey's check. Red grabbed it. "I'll take that," he said. He turned to Jimmy. "Well, buddy, every time some lush asks you to play 'Melancholy Baby' just once more . . . every time you can't get home because you're playing some dive on New Year's Eve . . . every time you knock yourself out on those one-night stands in Iowa and risk your neck racing to the next . . . think of good ol' Red—the fellow who made it."

He waved his hand in a grand gesture. "So long, slaves." He took Bobbie's and Dorothy's arms and guided them swiftly toward the cashier.

Watching them go, Dorsey shook his head in disbelief. "Who would have thought that Red would make it?" he said to Tony. "Guess he played it smart."

"Yeah," Tony said hollowly.

"You know, Tony," Dorsey went on. "I been thinking. If I got rid of my manager . . ."

Tony quickly stopped him. "You wouldn't want me," he said. "I'm unreliable."

At the cash register, Red stared numbly at the check

in his hand. He hadn't tried to act the big shot like this for twenty years. He reached for his wallet and whispered in Bobbie's ear simultaneously. "How much you got with you?"

Bobbie handed him her purse. "Sing 'Melancholy Baby,'" she said.

Red took the purse and turned quickly, hiding it against his chest. He paid the check and they went down the street to a hamburger stand. There they ate lunch in silence. Finished eating, Red said, "Now wasn't that better than eating where everybody knows you? I don't see how those *other* celebrities stand people staring at them."

"I do," Bobbie said. "I'll explain it to you some day." She took out of her purse the old photographs of the house which she had used to get Dorothy's interest in the hospital and laid them on the table. "I telephoned the real-estate man. We can get it for a song."

"I don't sing either," Red said. "And haven't you been the busy one with the telephone?"

"Dad, you promised," Dorothy said. She put her hand on his arm.

"The doctor said Los Angeles would be better for her," Bobbie reminded.

Red pointed out the window of the little hamburger stand. A yellow-gray mist was settling about telephone poles and buildings, reducing visibility. "That was the doctor up north," Red said. "He hasn't seen this smog." He looked at Dorothy, saw that she was breathing heavily. "This stuff isn't good for you. It isn't good for people who are well. It burns my eyes, nose and chest. People are going to drop dead like flies here some day."

"And you don't want to go back into music." Bobbie's tone was a line drawn under his words.

"And I don't want to go back into music."

He was kidding himself and he knew it. He knew that Bobbie knew he knew it.

But Bobbie didn't push him. She went on back up to San Leandro with him. She would wait for the moment when she knew he would bring the matter up again himself.

The moment came one evening when Red was fixing himself a bedtime snack in the kitchen—a huge, tripledecker sandwich. The flabby English bulldog watched, wagging his tailless rear end, waiting for part of it. Dorothy sat at the kitchen table in her nightgown, having a glass of milk. Bobbie, also seated, was having a cup of coffee. Red said, "Now if that Brown Derby down in Hollywood could make a sandwich like this . . ."

Bobbie realized he was thinking circuitously of Tony. "Have you heard any more from him?"

"No," Red replied. He blushed, realizing he had been trapped. "That's a great future you and Tony figured out for me. . . ."

Bobbie got up from the table. She went to him and took the sandwich. "Here—let me fix that. You've got everything in it but the dog."

"Blowing my brains out. Blowing my guts out. In some broken-down nightclub . . ."

"Built any good ships lately?" She was hitting below the belt.

"Look," he said. "You know the music business. It's

all different now. Nobody wants my kind of music."

"Lu Watters is doing all right at the Dawn Club. Over in the city. Why don't you go hear him?"

"I did."

"And?"

"The place is jumping all right. Some of the guys think the little hot Dixieland groups will come back."

"*Will?* They *are* back! Everywhere you read that swing is about finished. The big bands can't compete with the little combos."

"But most of them are playing—if you'll pardon the expression—the *new* jazz."

Bobbie handed him the sandwich. "Of course!" she exclaimed in mock agreement. "Anything new is better than old Dixieland and . . ."

"Now wait a minute." Red postponed biting the sandwich. "You know better than that. Dixieland has melody *and* rhythm. This experimental stuff just has—what does it have?"

Dorothy quit listening and set down her milk. "If I can put in my two cents' worth—give me Woody Herman," she said. "His trumpet section is the living end. He's getting a drummer who sends me. Ever hear of Dave Tough? He's been down in the South Pacific with Artie Shaw."

Bobbie's eyes met Red's. They smiled. *Dave Tough. Just the best jazz drummer the world ever knew.* Dorothy became aware of their exchange. "I know, I know," she said, holding up a hand. "He-played-in-father's-band."

"See?" Bobbie said to Red. "The Dixieland boys are still around, spreading the faith."

"Yeah, but how do I know people would like *my* Dixieland?"

"That never stopped you before." She put her coffee cup down heavily. "I've been sitting around here for years, waiting for you to punish yourself enough so you could go back to doing the only thing you're happy at . . . but you've been punishing yourself so long, you're beginning to like it!"

"Bobbie!" Red recoiled. He'd never heard her talk like this before.

Bobbie left the kitchen and returned with his old cornet. She shook it before him. "What happened to the wonderful lunatic I married? I don't know if your playing will be good, bad, or terrible. But I don't think that really matters. I want to get you out of that shipyard before we lose the war. I'm beginning to think I've lost mine!" She slammed down the cornet and started for the door. "You can sleep in that sandwich tonight," she called over her shoulder. "Pull the rye bread over you." She went out, slamming the door.

Dorothy got up to follow Bobbie, but stopped. She turned and looked sympathetically at her father.

Red got up and went to the icebox. He added a slab of cheese to his sandwich. "To keep my feet warm," he quipped.

"Dad?"

"Huh?"

"Why *did* you quit the music business?"

Red stuck his head in the icebox looking for salami. "I forget."

Dorothy walked over to him. She leaned down and kissed his cheek. "I guess I never even said 'thank you.'

I know what Mama meant about you punishing yourself. I can remember so many things now."

Red pulled his head away from the icebox, triumphantly dangling a piece of salami from thumb and forefinger. "So can I remember," he rattled, "the Ice Age . . . the Flood . . . Noah waving me aboard . . ."

"Would it be so tough for you to try to pick up where you left off?"

"You want to know the truth? Yes. I've laid off too long. My lip's gone. When that happens to a horn player, there's not a chance of coming back. It's impossible, that's all! In two words, im-possible!"

Dorothy walked over to the kitchen table and leaned on it to support her tiring legs. "I remember once when I talked like that . . . you threw a hot blanket on me." She slapped the table. "Right here on this table!"

Red sighed, feeling a bitterness deep inside him. "There's a lot of your mother in you. You just don't understand. All these guys I started . . . now they're big-time band leaders. They'd be laughing up their sleeves."

Dorothy made one of Red's funny faces. "There was one kid on our block," she began, imitating her father's voice, "Meyer, the crier." She turned away from him. "Good night, Meyer." She started walking slowly toward the door. She turned and saw that Red was watching her limp, was listening to her heavy breathing. "Some of the kids still laugh at me," she said, going through the door.

Red watched her until she disappeared up the corridor. He looked at the cornet lying in the corner where Bobbie threw it. He went over and picked it up. He pressed its three valves rapidly in succession. They were stiff. So were his fingers. For a long time he stood there working the pistons, loosening them. He compressed his lips and imagined himself blowing a high C. Then he pressed two of the valves down and made the same mental C with a different color, after his "false-fingering" style which had influenced so many cornet and trumpet players, even Beiderbecke. In his mind, he could form the notes perfectly.

He looked about him to see that no one was watching. He put the cup-shaped mouthpiece to his lips, tightened his diaphragm and blew. He hit the note right on the nose. He blew again and again, running the scale. The bulldog, having given up hope of getting some of his sandwich, had gone to sleep beside the warm oven of the kitchen stove. Hearing the cornet, he growled in his sleep.

Bobbie stopped putting cream on her face and came out of her bedroom. Dorothy appeared at her doorway. Both looked down the corridor, then at one another, faintly smiling. They listened as riffs and triple-tonguing effects rolled from Red's horn, and exchanged looks of relief and delight. Then Red hit a sour note, flat and coarse. The bulldog whined. Bobbie and Dorothy moved toward one another for comfort. Had they done the wrong thing in encouraging him? Hardly breathing, they waited. Again the right notes came. A couple of bars from "Indiana," a line from "Ida, Sweet as Apple Cider." Again the clinkers jarred the house. Again the dog whined. But again and again Red tried, the tones improving. Smiling, Bobbie motioned for Dorothy to go back to bed.

CHAPTER 12

ORCHESTRA LEADER Henry Busse was playing the Palace Hotel in San Francisco. He came down with the 'flu. He asked the musicians' union to recommend a good leader to substitute for him. The union told him about Red Nichols who was working over in Alameda in the shipyard. Busse knew that Red, first and nearly always a Dixieland man, could, however, play anything.

Busse telephoned Red. Red thought it was a joke or a plot. "Sure, I'll lead for you," he said. "And if you have any broken horns I also weld." When he found out Busse was on the level, he panicked. "My lip," he said. "I'm out of practice."

"So don't play," Busse said. "Front for me."

More nervous than when he was playing in his father's ladies' band, Red took a leave of absence from his job and stood up for Busse.

It was a good feeling being up there again in front of all those people, feeling the soft warmth of the spotlight on his face, instead of a white-hot torch, hearing the polite clapping instead of the cacophony of the shipyard. Through set after set he conducted impeccably, nice music for nice people. Time after time his eyes went to the trumpet in the hands of Busse's man. How he would like to grab that horn and bust out with some gut bucket!

If he had a lip.

He resisted the impulse. Blow clinkers at this crowd and he'd never live it down.

Busse got well and Red went back to the shipyard. Now he knew he could never be happy there, that he had to play again. The first evening that he came home from the shipyard, he announced that he was going to drive out to the edge of town and walk the dog through the hills before dinner.

After he had left the house, Bobbie discovered that his cornet was gone. When he returned home she had to use the car to go to the market. As she backed out of the driveway she felt something bump her ankle. It was the cornet. She stopped and examined it. The pipes were damp. She put the cornet back in its place and urged him to walk that fat dog every night.

Night after night Red and the dog left the house. Outside of town, in the rolling green hills, he stopped the car and took his stance on a knoll overlooking a ravine. There he practiced scales, riffs, runs and long tones, his eye on the dog, his ear tuned to the opposite bank, listening to the sounds come back, as he had listened for them to bounce off the mountains around Ogden and off the skyscrapers on his first trip to New York. At first the dog whined at his clinkers and waddled away, snuffling through the underbrush. In time, it tired of exploring and came and lay down beside Red, rolling its big black eyes up at him as the music poured from the horn. Before many days had gone by the dog sat beside him, leaning heavily against Red's leg as was his affectionate custom, listening with nary a complaint.

"If the dog can take it, the cats should, too," said Red, after one of these al fresco practice sessions. He took the dog home and announced that he wouldn't be walking it any more. "He's in pretty good shape now," he told Bobbie.

"And what shape are you in?" She gave him a long, affectionate smile.

"You know?"

"And I'm proud."

He told her he had paid up with the musicians' union, and planned to sit in a few evenings with a small combo in Oakland. "If they don't throw me out, I'll call Tony," he said.

"Good," Bobbie said. "I told him a few days ago that you would."

For that he spanked her on the fanny.

It was not easy. His wind was weak and he lacked the power for the high notes. When he did manage to hit them, his hernia gave him trouble. His fingering was rusty on the fast numbers and he hit plain wrong notes time and again. Yet the kids in the combo, being bad themselves, thought he was great. "You're Red Nichols, aren't you? You gotta be great," the pianist explained. They took to following his lead—all three of them—piano, bass fiddle and sax. Slowly, steadily, he improved. Before long, he was lecturing them for their mistakes, demanding that they learn their instruments better, learn to read.

Finally one day he telephoned Tony in L. A. Tony's secretary said he was in Acapulco, but that she would tell him Red called. Days went by without word from Tony. Red wouldn't tell Bobbie that he had tried to reach Tony. He was sure Tony was giving him the runaround. A couple weeks later he tried telephoning him again. "I'm sorry," Tony's girl said. "Mr. Valani has gone to Europe. He won't be back for three months. What? Yes. I sent all his messages to Acapulco."

Big shot Tony. Touring the world. Running around with movie stars and television stars. He didn't have time for a broken-down Dixieland cornet player. Success had gone to his head. Sure, call me up sometime. Good to hear from you, man. Let's get together, huh? How about lunch sometime? Don't call me, I'll call you. Yeah, but what have you done for me recently?

Red had never let anybody know how broken up he had been the time he lost his great band to Goodman. Now he certainly wouldn't whine about a lousy agent not returning a telephone call. He'd go out and make it on his own. Like he had two times before—first, in building up to a top pit band on Broadway, then in building up again from scratch to a top radio band.

"Don't you think it's time to make that call to Tony?" Bobbie suggested one afternoon when he came home from the shipyards.

"Not going to call him," Red said, avoiding her eyes. "I'm going out and put together a band like that time in Nebraska. Remember?"

"How can I forget? You tried to wiggle out of it, young man."

In a way, he knew that this was what he needed. He couldn't ask for favors. He had to make his own way. If his music was good, people would listen. If it wasn't, they wouldn't. It was that simple. And that was how it should be. Did a farmer ask friends to praise his tomatoes? No. He showed them. If they were good, people bought them.

Now he became the Red Nichols of old. He hammered at those Oakland kids until they wished they'd never heard of him. Using them as a nucleus, he brought in a trombone player and a drummer to wake them up.

One night Nick Bourne, a reporter for the United Press, heard the band and recognized Red. "Man, all you need is some publicity and you'll tootle right back up there," Nick said. "I'm just the character who can give it to you 'cause I'm having a brain storm. And when I have a brain storm it blows somebody sumpin'."

Thereupon Nick unfolded his scheme. "A colleague who shall remain nameless—because he's a no-good bastard—has put a bug in my ear. He said, 'Get a load of this,' but I said, 'No, I've got a load—just give me the bug.' Well, he said the fair little town of Albany, Calif., which has a stinking waterfront was overrun with stinking wharf rats and why didn't I do something about it. For the papers, that is. So I'm going to take action. You dress up like Pie-Eyed Piper or a rat terrier—I mean a Pied Piper—and come atootin' down the waterfront and pipe the rats over into Berkeley where the folks have more money and can afford to feed them."

Red knew a good publicity stunt when he heard it. Once he had passed out red nickels in Columbus, Ohio, to advertise himself until someone suggested that even nail polish might be considered illegal defacing. Another time he consented to pose for a photograph of himself trying to mail a chain letter—a letter with fifty pounds of chain wrapped around it.

"The original 'Pied Piper of Hamelin' blew three shrill notes," he was quoted as saying in Bourne's advance story. "Eminent psychologists say that rats respond to high-pitched sounds, but they don't hear low ones at all. I propose to hit a high note with overtones in the super audible range to get these rats that steal our chickens and raise the dickens.

"I'll give them a come-hither note that will make them want to do a maypole dance. I'll pipe them on down the avenue without a single thing to do, but lead the rats away and let them drown in Frisco Bay."

For this stunt, Bobbie whipped up a little pointed hat and a weskit for him. While the Albany Chamber of Commerce applauded and pedestrians held their sides, Red Nichols and his Pied Pipers played their first and last performance on the streets of Albany. Bourne's highly imaginative story of the highly imaginative incident was widely printed and motion picture newsreels featured shots of Red, grinning from ear to ear, stepping high, playing his cornet two-handed like a piper's flute, down the main street of Albany.

Musicians who had long thought him dead sent him

clippings along with their good wishes to the Albany Chamber of Commerce. Among them was a suggestion from an old friend that Glen Gray might be able to use him in his Casa Loma band.

Red got in touch with Gray. Gray always had admired Red's playing and was glad to have him, soft lip or not. If Red accepted he would have to go to New York. He asked Bobbie what she thought about it. "It's a chance," she said. "We'll miss you. But if you do okay, remember, Tony is waiting."

"Good, let him wait," Red said.

In February, 1944, Red went to New York and took his place in Gray's band. If his playing lacked anything, nobody but he noticed it. He made a half dozen recordings with Gray, cut discs that went to Army men overseas and played in a memorial to Bix Beiderbecke.

In five months he brought his lip back. But this was not what he wanted, playing here and there in other people's dance bands for whatever they would pay. This was not leading his own band, his own Five Pennies, playing his own Dixieland jazz. One night, just as he was about to throw in the sponge and go back home to San Leandro, to welding, Red got a telephone call from Tony, in Hollywood.

"Sweetheart!" Tony exclaimed. "I heard you on a Decca disc. Why didn't you tell me? You're ready! Come home fast. Everybody's asking about you."

"How were things in Acapulco?" Red asked pointedly.

"Whaddaya mean, Acapulco? I been everywhere," Tony exclaimed.

"I sent a message to you by your secretary."

"Never got it, doll. That broad was in love. She got married and walked out, leaving everything snafued."

"So what do you want from me?"

"Look, Red. I can't promise you a big show in Vegas or anything like that. But I got a little night spot where you can make a start. You pull 'em in there, we go on to bigger things."

Red got his release from Gray and went home. Was Bobbie game? Did the doctor really think Los Angeles and its chest-searing smoke and fumes would be better for Dorothy? Bobbie was game. The doctor hedged. "Dorothy would be better off in a warmer climate, not necessarily Los Angeles."

Red decided to move far out in a Los Angeles suburb, outside the smog belt.

As they prepared to leave San Leandro, his father, long lingering at the joint of death, breathed his last.

"You must be joyful because my work is done. Why should there be tears on the end of your nose? Make no monument for me. Carve no stone. If you must mark my grave, put the shoes that I worked in at the head. Let the run-down heels and the hole in the soles say that I worked hard and did my best. Be grateful that my work and my mission is finished. Be joyful and play happy music."

Red buried his father—his teacher—a piece of his heart—and went south to play happy music.

An illuminated banner of the little downtown hotel nightspot proclaimed:

TONIGHT!
TRIUMPHANT RETURN!
RED NICHOLS
AND
HIS FIVE NEW PENNIES

But the parking attendant asleep on his little canvas stool out front told a not-so-triumphant story.

Inside the plain little joint, Bobbie and Dorothy sat at a small circular table directly in front of the bandstand, tense and expectant, acutely aware that the place was only half filled. Behind the darkened bandstand, Red, dapper in a tuxedo, his gray hair neatly combed, peered through the partly open curtain at the small crowd. Beside him, Tony patted him on the shoulder, and gulped at the small crowd. The band members, all dressed neatly and alike in the decorous fashion that Red demanded of other Pennies over the years, ducked out and started taking their places.

"My name outside certainly pulled them in," Red said. "I can get a bigger crowd to watch a welding torch."

"It's early yet," Tony, behind him, said.

Red shook his head sadly. "No, Tony. It's late. It's awfully late. But I did think a few fellow dinosaurs would show up. If only to see how long it took me to crack my lip again." He counted the house in that smiling way that told no one what he was doing. "Twenty-one. Counting the bartender. The twenty probably are his relatives. You know, a lot of sorehead musicians used to come around where I played just waiting to hear me hit a clinker. They hated me for trying to make them be perfect. I never hit one for them. If they came tonight maybe I could accommodate them." He turned his back on the audience. "Where's the Red Nichols fan clubs?"

Tony pointed to Bobbie and Dorothy sitting out front. "There's the best fan club you ever had. I'd give all the willing waitresses in Hoboken for two like 'em."

"Don't get me wrong. Why do you think I want to go over? For myself? Ha!"

"You don't think I got you this job just because of *you*? Man, I envy you those two sweethearts out there. Guess I never told you that before. All the time on the road, you thought I was having all the fun while you were tied down with your companionate baby. I just want you to know that I really thought you were the luckiest guy in the world. I still think so." He took his lapels in thumb and forefinger. "Look at me. Hundred and fifty dollar suit. Shoes from England. Closets full of everything, including girls. So what am I trying to prove? You tell me. Next time I go east I may stop off in Brooklyn, like you did. Who knows?"

Tony slapped Red on the shoulder in a parting gesture and stepped down onto the dance floor. He gave a signal and, as the house lights dimmed, he walked over and sat down with Red's beautifully gowned, excitement-flushed wife and daughter. The curtains parted on the darkened bandstand. The bass drum began a beat. A light came on inside it, revealing the familiar legend:

RED NICHOLS
AND
THE FIVE PENNIES

A spotlight picked up the bell of Red's cornet, then widened to include Red himself playing the opening bars of his theme song, "Wail to the Wind."

As Tony sat down beside her, Bobbie saw that he was frowning. She thought he didn't like the sound of Red's horn. "He's been practicing and practicing . . ." Her voice trailed off.

Red was trying hard but failing to stop the rattling of dishes and glasses. He became aware of the sounds and blew harder. It was no use. He could work as a sideman but to lead his own band, you had to have something distinctive that people want. He'd had it once. He didn't have it now. Funny how the noises out there reminded him of other noises from bandstands. The first time an audience grew silent while he played it scared him to death. They remained silent at the finish and he thought they hadn't liked him. Then a wave of applause had broken over the house. What he would give for that now!

Suddenly he heard a trumpet, as though from that house of long ago. A smattering of applause, not loud enough to interrupt it but loud enough to encourage, accompanied it.

The trumpet came on louder. Red lowered his cornet to listen, spellbound, dazed. His temples throbbed. He thought he was going to faint. He was hearing things. Ghosts. Louis Armstrong's trumpet?

No. Not ghosts. A voice. A voice that seemed to come from deep in a gravel pit. "Won't you come home, Bill Bailey? Won't you come home?," it was singing. Louis' voice.

Red turned. Through the darkness of the club, toward the door, he saw a flashing golden trumpet. Then a dark head, glistening with perspiration, white teeth shining, coming toward him. There was no mistaking these sights and sounds. Red raised his voice toward Louis and sang back at him, his heart in his mouth, "I'm feelin' all alone."

An alert electrician picked up Louis with a light and led him slowly toward the bandstand. "Won't you come home, Bill Bailey? Won't you come home?" It became a duet.

Harlem . . . prohibition booze in cups . . . his first date with Bobbie . . . stepping on her feet . . . "Battle Hymn of the Republic" . . . "glory, glory, hallelujah" . . . "Get that boy's license number . . . He caught the nightingale" . . . Memories crowded Red's brain. Through tear-glazed eyes he watched Louis come on toward him. Now the music seemed bigger, richer. Wasn't that Jimmy Dorsey's saxophone? Red peered beyond the big, dark glistening head of Armstrong and made out Dorsey behind him, blowing up a storm, trying to keep his lips straight and not grin up at Red, but saying "Hello, friend" with his eyes. Dave Tough, too. Little Dave. No drum with him but hitting everything in sight with his sticks in perfect, syncopated rhythm.

The front door to the club was open and people

streamed in behind the marching musicians. At their table, Tony, Bobbie and Dorothy were as amazed as Red. Now they led the crowd in applauding.

Red tried to play on, but could not, overcome by it all. One by one the visitors stepped up onto the bandstand with his Pennies, Louis, Jimmy, Dave.

"Bill Bailey" finished and the newcomers moved into "Indiana," the new Pennies quickly following.

Red motioned to Bobbie. "Come up here," he said, into the microphone. "I want the *whole* band."

Tony pushed the unwilling Bobbie toward the bandstand. She stepped up, beaming. "They're wonderful," she said. Red leaned toward her, a hand to his mouth. "Someday they'll all be working for *me*." Bobbie kissed the musicians as she moved around to take her place with Red and Louis at the microphone.

"Come on, honey," Louis rumbled. "Belt it out."

Bobbie put a hand to her lips. "I don't think I can." She looked at Red. "I'm a little misty-eyed tonight. Too misty-eyed. But I do have a surprise for you."

Red's head snapped back. "You couldn't be! Show me the rabbit!"

Bobbie was looking beyond him. "Dorothy—" she said, motioning to the child.

Slowly Dorothy was walking toward them, inspired by the excitement to out-do herself. She had left her cane at the table and she walked without braces. Flat-footed and hesitantly at first, but she was walking without artificial aid.

Red caught Bobbie's signal and turned. He leaped from the bandstand then, slowing down, walked casually to meet Dorothy. When he was directly in front of her, she looked up at him and said, "May I have this dance?"

Dorsey saw what was happening and quickly signaled for a change of tempo. He took the lead into a lullaby that Red used to sing to Dorothy in the days when she was interrupting poker games by staying up. Tough fell in with him while Louis and the new Pennies listened. Then they joined in as Bobbie sang the words.

Red took Dorothy's right hand in his left and put his right hand behind her back. Slowly he began to dance with her. One could see it was an effort for her but she moved with him without hesitation. Midway in the dance, Red picked her up from the floor and held her in his arms. He carried her up onto the bandstand, his heart swelling with joy.

Dorothy tapped his shoulder. "Put me down," she exclaimed. "I can stand on my own two feet."

Red put her down. "So," he said, "can I." He held out his hand to her. "Ala Kazam, Kazam," he said, and gave her their old blood brother handshake.

From the closed door at the far end of the huge motion picture sound stage, Red could barely hear the actors' dialogue. When the bell sounded twice and the red light at the door went off, he pushed the door open and went out.

He had lived a good third act.

Dorothy had completely recovered, except for some occasional breathing difficulty, and married a hard-working boy named David Mason who was doing well as a land appraiser and they had presented Red and Bobbie with three wonderful grandchildren.

Red had built a fine home in suburban Glendale with a swimming pool and Dorothy's family had moved there close to him and Bobbie. Because Southern California's infamous smog was getting worse, impairing Dorothy's breathing, Bobbie and Red were selling out and moving to a new home up in the desert where Dorothy could come to escape the choking smoke and fumes during smog alerts.

Not only could Red stand on his own feet, as the movie said, but he was going places. After the comeback engagement, the Five Pennies moved into a Hollywood night spot, then another, and played long engagements at swank spots in Phoenix, Palm Springs, Lake Tahoe, Reno and Las Vegas. When they weren't playing those, Red and/or some of the Pennies were on radio or television with John Scott Trotter, Ray Noble, the Andrews Sisters, Ginny Sims, Charley McCarthy, Bing Crosby or George Gobel. Since 1945, Red's horn has been heard on dozens of records backing singers like Crosby, Phil Harris, Ella Fitzgerald, Allan Jones, Julia Lee, Jesse Price and Frank Sinatra, as well as with the Pennies on their own records. As in the old days when he recorded under various names, he is billed as Red Nichols and His Five Pennies; Loring (Red) Nichols and His Syncopated Chamber Music; Red Nichols and His Pennies; Red Nichols Trio; Red Nichols and His Famous Pennies; Red Nichols and His Penny Symphony; Red Nichols and His New Orchestra.

In 1951 NBC honored him with an hour's program called "Silver Plus Five," with nearly every jazz musician of note participating. In 1956 he was the subject of Ralph Edwards' television show, "This Is Your Life," on which old-timers like Miff Mole appeared.

In fact, Nichols' comeback has become as big as he wants it. Like himself, his Pennies are all gray-haired, but jumping. They are Rollie Culver, drums; Pete Beilmann, trombone; Billy Wood, clarinet; Joseph (Blizzard Head) Rushton, Jr., bass sax; Jean Plummer, piano.

They play everything—unobtrusive dinner music, cha-chas; waltzes, rock 'n' roll, or Dixieland gut bucket—whatever the people or the places call for.

At this writing still bigger things are in store for him. A television show is being planned, and he's buying bags in prepara-

tion for what promises to be a triumphal European tour, judging by interest there in his records.

As Louis Armstrong said, "Red Nichols is going to be a bigger cat than ever."

SPECIAL OFFER TO READERS OF THIS BOOK

If you have enjoyed this book—and would like to have a list of the other fine Dell Books available in inexpensive paperbound editions—you can receive a copy of our latest catalogue by sending your name and address to Dell Books Catalogue Department, 321 West 44th Street, New York 36, N. Y.

A DELL FIRST EDITION

Darby O'Gill
and The Little People

by Lawrence Edward Watkin

*A heart-warming story
for the entire family—
about mortals and leprechauns
at the eternal battle of wits.
The result is a topsy-turvy world
of laughter and delight.*

A Walt Disney Production

If this book cannot be obtained locally, send 25c (plus 5c for postage and handling) for each copy to Dell Publishing Co., Inc., 321 West 44th Street, New York 36, N. Y. If order is for five or more books, no postage or handling charge is required.